CW00953623

TWENTY GREAT WALKS
from
BRITISH RAIL

Les Lumsdon
&
Colin Speakman

Sigma Press - Wilmslow

First published in 1987 by:
Sigma Press, 98a Water Lane, Wilmslow, SK9 5BB, England.

Printed in Malta by Interprint Limited

ISBN: 1 85058 099 5

British Library Cataloguing in Publication Data

Lumsdon, Les
    Twenty Great Walks from British Rail
    1. Walking -- Great Britain -- Guide books 2. Great Britain --
    Description and Travel -- 1971- -- Guide books
    I. Title II. Speakman, Colin
    941.1′04858   DA650

Acknowledgment: we gratefully acknowledge the cooperation of British Rail during the preparation of this book; the British Rail logo is reproduced with permission.

Illustrations: these are by Beverley Gowing, a freelance illustrator and designer from Pontefract, Yorkshire.

Maps: designed by David Holdsworth, from Rastrick, Halifax. The maps are based upon the appropriate Ordnance Survey maps with the permission of the Controller of Her Majesty's Stationery Office. Crown Copyright reserved.

Cover: by David Collins of Professional Graphics, Warrington.

The Twenty Great Walks

Map of selected rail lines showing links with walking routes and mainline system.

Inverness

20

19

Aberdeen

18

17

Edinburgh

Glasgow

Carlisle

12 Newcastle

10 Darlington

11

9 York

Leeds

Doncaster

Manchester

Liverpool

8 Sheffield

16 Chester

Crewe

15

Shrewsbury

7 Grantham

Norwich 4

6 Birmingham

14

Hereford 5

13 Cardiff Oxford

Swansea

London

Portsmouth

Exeter 3

Plymouth 2 Eastbourne

1

An Introduction

No land on earth can match Britain for the sheer dazzling variety of its landscapes. Everything from the wildest, bleakest mountains to the gentlest wood and parkland, from storm-lashed cliffs to the softest sandy beaches, from long level marshes to luxuriant, sub-tropical gardens, is to be found in this one small island. And add to this its countless fascinating cities, towns and villages, some of them dating from Roman times, many of them medieval, lots of them still dominated by gracious Georgian or Regency houses and terraces, many of them echoing the confident exuberance of the Victorians when Britain was the centre of the world's largest Empire, and you have a country which, for all its industrialisation and urbanisation, can still amaze and delight.

But if all this isn't enough, Britain has two other matchless assets. The first is its footpath network. Originally created in Anglo-Saxon times and enshrined in the ancient, common law of the land, our rights of way evolved from the beaten earth paths that ran from settlement to settlement, supplemented over the centuries by monastic packhorse tracks, drove roads and pre-turnpike highways. They are as old as our civilisation, fragments of living history, which are, in turn, a marvellous way of enjoying that history, penetrating deep into a countryside which has evolved around them.

There's no finer way of experiencing the countryside than from a footpath. When you walk a path you are a part of the landscape, not separate from it as in a motor vehicle, but close to the scents, the sounds, the moods of the natural world, able to see, to observe, to read the landscape in all its complex variety. Much that has been lost to 20th century man roaring past on the super-highway can be regained by the quiet rambler.

So often the beauty of our landscape is a soft, subtle beauty, not one which immediately opens all its secrets, but something to come upon almost unawares - a sudden glimpse of a stream through the leaves of a tree, the colour of an autumn moorland, a frozen waterfall in the depths of winter, the soft flapping of a heron across a lake, a medieval church tower rising above an October mist.

Using your Railway

That other marvellous, undervalued, asset of Britain's countryside is our railway network. Britain was, of course, the great railway pioneering country - Stockton & Darlington, Liverpool & Manchester are engraved in every text book of the Industrial and Technological Revolution that has changed the world. But railways, too, had a profound influence on the shaping of our own landscape, not just in the lines, stations, viaducts and bridges themselves, but in the kind of social changes, the growth of villages, suburbs and market towns which helped to transform a purely rural community into one which was a far greater mix of rural and urban. It created whole new towns, particularly the Victorian seaside resorts, and brought the tourist industry into being. It is no coincidence that Thomas Cook, one of the world's first great travel agents, started out on his huge enterprise by organising trips by train.

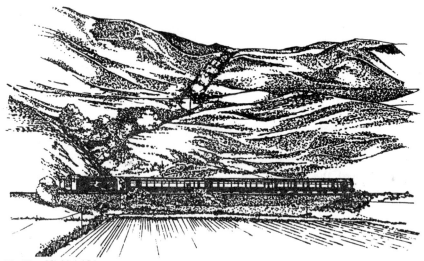

The West Highland Line

Most significantly for this book, it was the railways gradually extending their tentacles deep into the countryside which first made it possible for city dwellers to get out to enjoy that countryside in ever increasing numbers.

Only a few years ago, it was assumed that in rural areas at least, the motor car had virtually wiped out the need for railways in the countryside. Politicians and planners assumed that all that was needed was a handful of main line railways to and from London.

And yet, in the late 1980s, country railways in Britain are enjoying a remarkable revival. Lines, once destined for closure, have enjoyed a quite dramatic increase in passenger revenue, often through community initiative and enterprise which British Rail has matched with imaginative marketing campaigns, even, on occasions, leading to the reopening of long-closed country stations for a new generation of regular passengers.

What this proves is something which politicians are coming to understand. People like railways, as a comfortable, safe, and pleasant way of travelling, equally open to both sexes and all age groups, irrespective of income. The view from a railway carriage window is a good way of enjoying the landscape or townscape, often from unfamiliar angles, free of the roadside ribbon development that spoils many trunk roads, and the concrete monotony of most motorways. Drivers too can travel free of the stress, strain and sheer boredom of a crowded road system.

Little wonder the Government has now recognised the importance of railways for that most important of growth industries - tourism. Railways are recognised as being a part of our national heritage and, equally significantly, are a marvellous way, especially for many thousands of visitors from overseas, of enjoying that heritage.

Of course, in one sense, trains aren't as flexible as cars. You must plan your journey in advance, consulting timetables, work out your return trip, judge distance carefully. But, with the BR national timetable to hand, this can be part of the fun. And in some ways the train can be more flexible and offer more freedom than the car. The car driver is attached by an invisible umbilical cord to his parked vehicle, to which he must return. The rail traveller is a free agent. He can, as this book will suggest, return from an entirely different point along the route, no longer limited to the tiresome circular walk dictated by the car. Walking from station to station is one of the delights of using the train.

About the Walks

This book then, is intended to be an introduction to using Britain's railway system as a means of enjoying that heritage, of discovering the real beauty of the countryside. We've taken 20 walking routes, ranging from 6 to 15 miles, throughout Great Britain, taking Scotland and Wales and separate sections, and dividing England into three major regions - North, the Midlands and the South. Northern Ireland has been omitted because of lack of space.

We've written the book for three kinds of people. Firstly, for those who love Britain's countryside and want to explore it without being dependent, for whatever reason, on the car. Secondly there are those people who happen to enjoy travelling by train but would like to add extra purpose to the rail trip, getting out at one or more of those tempting little stations and discovering what lies at the end of the station drive. This book is full of tempting little stations. Thirdly, it's for the many visitors to Britain, perhaps armed with a Brit Rail Pass, Inter-Rail or the host of Regional Rover tickets who, would like to escape from the kind of cliches about Britain - Beefeaters, Bearskins and Bagpipes - which are so often peddled in tourist brochures, and discover something a little different, and rather more special. This book is a little bit of the real England, Wales and Scotland.

What makes a "Great" walk ? Our choice is inevitably subjective, but each walk we chose, often after repeated visits and careful research, had to have some outstanding quality - either landscape or historical associations, and preferably both, which would be both typical of the region it was in, and give a real flavour of the best Britain has to offer. Above all, it had to be a good walk. Of course, our choice isn't intended to be definitive or exhaustive - we could have very easily had twenty walks for each of our chosen countries or regions. In many cases, it was dictated by questions of balance and practicality and there are plenty more walks to be discovered, even finer than those here, all easily done by using the train.

Some Practical Points

We have tried to give the basic, essential information for each walk, including the starting and finishing station and, where possible, a halfway or intermediate point where you can curtail the walk in case of emergency or bad weather. What you won't find is exact train times. These change too frequently to be of value, and whilst we would say that at the time of writing there was a good, basic train service from which to do this particular walk, and in most cases a choice of trains, you must check exact times with that invaluable compendium of information, the British Rail National Passenger Timetable which, if it is too bulky for pocket or rucksack, can make marvellous bedtime reading for anyone with a whiff of railway romance about them. Sundays are often a problem on less busy country lines, though a surprising number of quite rural lines mentioned in the text have very good Sunday services during the summer months.

Use an Ordnance Survey map. We have tried, in our walk descriptions, to describe the route as accurately as we can. The sketch maps, prepared from evidence on the ground, are a guide. Inevitably, it's an impossible task to avoid inaccuracies and ambiguities, as words are a blunt tool and the countryside is a rapidly changing place. Things that were there when this book was researched, may well vanish overnight as walls get knocked down, barns are demolished, roads are widened and trees felled. We can only apologise for such things in advance. With a large scale map however, you have a better chance, as the basic topography doesn't change. Learn how to read the map (mainly applied common sense) and work from the map to the words rather than the other way round. Remember, the sketch maps in the book are for broad guidance only.

We have suggested at the very minimum an Ordnance Survey 1:50,000 scale Landranger Map (available from all larger bookshops and outdoor specialists - look for the magenta cover) or, if at all possible, either the excellent new (green) Pathfinder 1:25,000 or larger (yellow) Outdoor Leisure Maps - the latter mainly for National Park or other popular walking areas. These larger scale 1:25,000 maps offer superb, exact detail, including field walls, which make them perhaps the best walking maps in the world. They are usually available locally, from bookshops or Tourist Information Centres.

Decent footwear is essential for all these walks, either standard walking boots or the new lightweight fell boots. You might get away with stout shoes on some of the routes, but mud is endemic on most British footpaths most times of the year. Town shoes can vanish into mud and bogs with alarming ease, whilst boots give that essential ankle support over rougher country and can prevent a strain or a even a break. Always carry rainwear - the British climate is notoriously fickle - a spare sweater and emergency supplies of food and drink. In hill country, it is sensible to carry a compass, whilst in the winter months it is foolish to go out without a torch. Always leave word where you are going and when you are expected back, and it's probably a sensible precaution to have enough money with you - cash, plastic or cheque - to buy an overnight's accommodation in the unlikely event of you missing the last return train.

On every one of these walks, please treat the life and work of the countryside with respect, keeping, whenever possible, to footpaths, and taking all litter home with you. Remember the old adage for respecting the natural world - "take only photographs - leave only footprints."

Grades of Walks

A word about our grading of each walk. "Easy" means that this is a walk suitable for people who are not experienced walkers, is fairly level, uses easy-to-find paths and is likely to be attractive to families with children who are reasonably energetic. "Moderate" assumes that you can cope with longer distances, steeper gradients, slightly more difficult pathfinding and places where the going is a little more difficult. Older children will cope with such routes, providing they have some experience. "Strenuous" - and this is reserved for only a couple of walks in this book - means that there are stretches of rough going, perhaps steep and boggy and places where pathfinding needs some care and skill - particularily when there's a train to catch. For this grade of walk, you must be well equipped, used to pathfinding with a compass and be prepared to cross a bit of rough country, including the occasional stream.

Thanks to BR...

Finally, may we express our gratitude to British Rail which has, at every level, been extremely helpful to us in our work - both in an official capacity in planning this book, and to us as ordinary travellers on the railway system. We travelled many thousands of miles whilst researching the walks, from the Scottish Highlands to Cornwall, from the Welsh Coast to the Norfolk Broads, and the standard of service we enjoyed was rarely less than excellent, with most trains running to time. We have a rail system to be proud of, and deserving, at every level, our fullest support.

Our gratitude must go, too, to various local authorities along the lines which, when approached about footpath and other matters, responded with immediate action, to our requests for help or information.

May their tourist trade prosper, and may those tourists come to walk their footpaths by train !

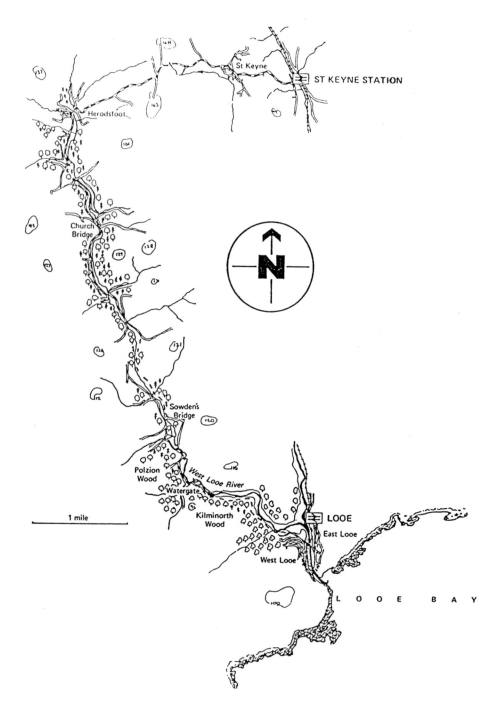

St Keyne

Herodsfoot

Church
Bridge

N

Sowden's
Bridge

Polzion
Wood

West Looe River

Watergate

Kilminorth
Wood

1 mile

☰ LOOE

East Looe

West Looe

L O O E   B A Y

8

WALK ONE: West Looe Valley

Landranger Map: Sheet 201

Pathfinder Map: Sheets SX 25/35 and SX26/36

Starting Station: St Keyne

Finishing Station: Looe

Distance: 9 miles (15 Km)

Time Required: 4 hours

Grade: Easy to Moderate.

Possible Cut-Off Point: Church Bridge 4 miles (6.5 Km) with a walk along lanes to Causeland Station.

Terrain: The walk begins along quiet and narrow Cornish lanes, into the West Looe valley, then along forest paths and green lanes to the coast.

Refreshment and Accommodation: Looe and Liskeard are both excellent centres.

Tourist Information: The Guildhall, Looe (050 36) 2072

THE RAIL JOURNEY

Any rail journey to England's South West is exquisite, through Somerset to the cathedral city of Exeter, then along the golden sweeping sands of Dawlish and Teignmouth. There is ever changing scenery to enjoy, from the broad expanses of the Somerset Levels to the Mendip Hills, to the fringes of Exmoor and Dartmoor National Parks, all countryside of great beauty and interest.

This is Great Western Railway territory.The GWR was perhaps the most glamorous railway company of them all, whose non-stop trains of milk, vegetables and fish from the fertile West Country to London and the Midlands, world-beating crack expresses "The Cornishman" and "Cornish Riviera", and handsome green and brass "King" and "Castle" steam locomotives are the stuff of legend.

It was the GWR that opened up the South Western holiday resorts, "The English Riviera", to the new market of Victorian holidaymakers from London, the Midlands and the North. In the 1980s and '90s GWR traditions live on in the form of British Rail whose InterCity trains still carry thousands of holidaymakers seeking the sun.

The West Looe Valley

Isambard Kingdom Brunel, one of the greatest British engineers of all time, built the high bridge over the River Tamar at Saltash - a masterpiece of engineering which signifies your arrival in Cornwall. Liskeard is the next stop to change onto the Looe branch. Its station is a good 5 minutes walk from the centre of town, a jumble of streets with a number of fine Georgian and Victorian buildings. Liskeard's importance, however, dates way back before the Railway Age to the 13th century when it was chartered as a "stannary" town. This meant that all tin smelted in nearby areas had to be brought in to be tested to ensure that quality standards were maintained. There's a local history museum outlining the area's history if you have time for a visit.

The line from Liskeard to Looe is fascinating, as for most of its length, it was built on the former Liskeard and Looe Union Canal. The railway was first opened from Moorswater (in a valley beneath Liskeard) to South Caradon and then Cheesewring. It was then extended to Looe in 1860 and only in 1879 did it begin to carry passengers. Not until 1901 did the Liskeard and Caradon Railway Company establish the unusual, almost horseshoe loop up to link with the line from London at Liskeard with a separate platform at right angles to the main line. You might even find it disconcerting at first and as the driver and guard reverse the train at Coombe for the scenic ride down the East Looe valley to the sea.

THE WALK

Alight at St Keyne, the first station after Coombe. Don't forget to tell the guard as this is a request stop. Once off the platform, turn left and immediately you come across Paul Corin's Musical Collection Centre. There are several instruments to hear - as well as see - French and German Carousel organs, Player Pianos and Orchestrions. Pass by the Centre and bear right at the first junction climbing up to St Keyne village. St Keyne was a 5th Century Welsh saint and it is said that he blessed the nearby Holy well in such a way that the husband or wife who first drinks the water will rule the roost for the remainder of the marriage. Fortunately for any married couples on this ramble, we are heading off in the other direction! Bear right at the junction in the village, then left just before the telephone kiosk. Follow this pleasant lane to the next junction with a rustic post box set back in the hedge. Go left here, then take the second turning on the right. This leads down to the quiet hamlet of Herodsfoot.

The West Looe Valley

Follow the lane over the West Looe River, by the Post Office and War Memorial, before taking the left turning to Pelynt. On the right you'll see the remains of Herodsfoot mine. The road enters woodland and at the next bridge across a tributary stream, bear left through a wooden gate into Pendruffle wood where silence reigns but for the ripple of the river. You come out onto a tarmac lane again. Continue ahead, but only for a very short distance. As the road bends to the left to Church Bridge your way is ahead once again into Duloe Wood. However, Church Bridge is the cut-off point for those wishing to shorten the walk by returning to Causeland Station. Follow the road over the bridge and climb up to Duloe village.Bear left and at Polvean Cross bear right and first right again to Badham Farm. Ignore the road leading in to the left, but turn left at the T-junction for the short walk to Causeland Station.

For those continuing, your way is along the forestry track alongside the river until a major junction is reached where you bear left to the ancient bridge, then follow a path which climbs up to the right above the flood plain before descending gently again towards the river.

This really is the heart of the lush and beautiful West Looe Valley, far from traffic and crowds. Immediately prior to the river bank, bear left over the wooden bridge and a stile. The right of way is shown on the map as leading up this secretive green lane to a point a few metres before it curves to the left sharply and becomes obstructed. Your path down the hillside to your right is a rough trod or earth track, which is none too clear, through the bracken, to a well-defined path below. Many people simply bear right at the bottom of the green lane and follow the lower path. Either way, the path keeps to the left of an ancient hedge at first then passes through it, across the brook, then leads towards a stile entering the wood. Your way is slightly to the right of the gate, then ahead towards the river, turning upwards again by the old forestry hut coming out at the top of the wood's edge. Continue forward along a hillside contoured path soon descending once again into another wood. The path is ahead, but be willing to walk around fallen trees and eroded hillside. As you approach the stream, bear left up the section of an old lane then right, over a stile and straight ahead again by passing the marshy ground on the right. At the tarmac lane, bear right over Sowden's Bridge then proceed along the lane bearing to the left; turn left at the first junction. Pass by a very isolated letter box in the moss and ivy covered walls. You'll also see the remains of old lime kilns.

Lime Kilns

At one time, sea, sand and seaweed were used to fertilize the land, being brought up by barge on the tidal section of the West Looe River to small wharves in this area.The sand was unloaded onto packhorses for the final journey to the fields, very often using green lanes like the ones seen earlier. As the landowners looked for improved methods, burnt lime (hydrated lime) came into favour. Limestone and coal needed for the kilns were transported by barge up the river just as the sand had been in previous times. So this would have been a far busier place than it is today.

The lane leads to the hamlet of Watergate. Bear left here onto a path through Kilminorth Wood with excellent views of grey herons and other wading birds in the river. As the path begins to descend towards the river, bear right upwards towards an ancient earthwork known as 'The Giant's Hedge', and at the junction go left down a number of steep steps to the boatyard where you bear right up the tarmac lane. A number of information boards along this part of the route illustrate local wildlife to be seen.

After a short distance, you reach a path leading off to the left which provides a pleasant approach to West Looe. Go through the car park to the bridge, then bear left on the other side for Looe station.

Looe

Looe is small but busy. Until the middle of last century, East and West Looe were virtually two separate communities. East Looe was famous for its fishing fleet and at times of war was called upon to provide extraordinarily large manpower and resources for its size. West Looe remained a sleepy village. As the fishing industry has declined on both banks of the river, so has tourism and holidaymaking taken over. You can find out more about the fascinating history of the area in a series of exhibitions in the town's Guildhall.

But if you fancy a dip in the sea after your walk, the safest beach is next to Banjo Pier, one minute from the centre. Smuggling, as every Daphne du Maurier devotee will tell you, was once part of life along this coast and although such illicit trade has now ceased, its legends and curios remain as part of the tourist industry.

But even the least Romantic is likely to want to seek out a suitable place of refreshment in the little town before a return rail trip. Whatever your taste you'll find plenty of choice, though if you can come outside the main holiday season, it'll be far less crowded. But then Looe is the kind of place which has a charm that appeals in all seasons.

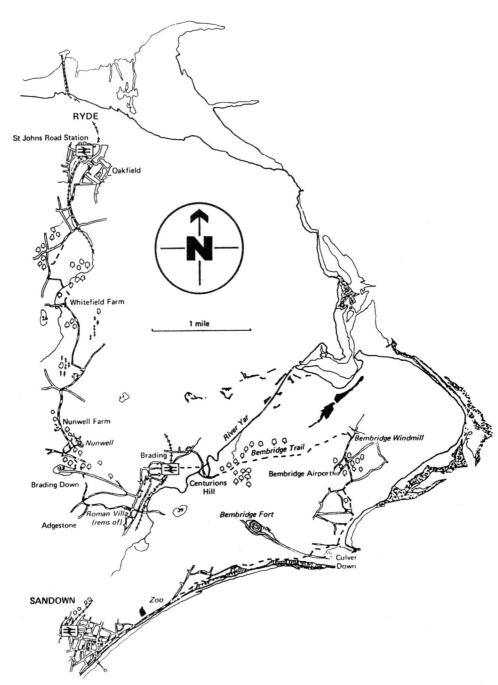

WALK TWO: Isle of Wight

Landranger Map: 196

Outdoor Leisure Map: 29

Starting Station: Ryde St John's Road

Finishing Station: Sandown

Distance: 11 miles (17.5km)

Time Required: 5 hours

Grade: Easy.

Possible Cut-Off Point: Brading 5 miles (9km)

Terrain: Gentle countryside and well-defined paths followed by a hillier coastal path.

Refreshment and Accommodation: Plentiful supply at Ryde and Sandown. Refreshment points on route. Youth hostel at Sandown.

Tourist Information: Western Esplanade, Ryde (0983) 62905 *or* The Esplanade, Sandown (0983) 403886

THE RAIL JOURNEY

There are several ways of crossing the Solent to the Isle of Wight, but for a connection with the Ryde to Shanklin electric railway, known as Ryde Rail, perhaps the best route is by way of Portsmouth Harbour and Ryde Pierhead. Sealink now use modern catamarans to ferry passengers the short distance to the island. It takes about 15 minutes and the service is designed to connect with the train to Shanklin. When your train arrives, it comes as a bit of a surprise to see ex-London Transport Underground trains on the electrified service !

The line is the sole survivor of a network of routes throughout the island. It was built in the early 1860s to ferry holidaymakers to the island's southern resorts - a function it still carries out. There was a later extension to Ventnor and a branch between Brading and Bembridge. Sadly, these are now closed.

THE ISLE OF WIGHT

The Isle of Wight is popular with holidaymakers. It has, after all one of the best sunshine records in the country and tends to be warmer than other places. It is also a friendly island. Local people seem to know how to cope with the summer influx and yet retain a civilised approach to the whole business - no mean achievement on an island of only 155 square miles with a population of about 115, 000 which swells substantially for eight to ten weeks each summer. There are endless attractions, ranging from the majestic Carisbrooke Castle and Osborne House, country home of Queen Victoria and Prince Albert, to the children's paradise of Blackgang Chine. The island's major asset, however, is its gently undulating landscape with a central chalk ridge and the more southerly downs plunging into the sea dramatically. Footpaths are clearly signed and well maintained, including routes to the sea, making the area a delight for the walker and a model to be followed by many a local authority elsewhere.

When you arrive in Ryde, at its half mile long pier built in 1824, it is easy to see its strategic location on the island as a crossing point. The town has a pleasant centre with a number of interesting buildings. Like Cowes, it is famous for its sailing and in particular, yachting. As a hobby, rambling perhaps comes a little cheaper!

THE WALK

Alight at St John's Road Station. Bear right at the station entrance, then right by the Oakfield Inn into High Street and then right again along Slade Road, signposted to Smallbrook Farm. Follow this bridleway, known as The Nunwell Trail, to the tarmac road (Smallbrook Lane). Bear right here and proceed with care to a point where the road bends right. Cross the road with caution to the footpath on the left and follow this round to the training ground where you bear right at the signpost for the barred gate in the corner of the field. Go through the gate and turn left on to Ashley Road. Soon, on the left, you reach a track signposted to Brading Down. Take this, continuing beyond the old railway track then bearing right to the farm. Go left by the milking shed and follow the track leading off with the hedge on your right then keeping to the left of the wood. Go through the barred gate with the hedge to your left at first, but then on your right in the next field, to the next gateway at the corner of the copse. Go through this and turn sharp left to the tarmac lane. Turn right and at the first junction go right again, then left along the drive towards Nunwell House.

Vineyards

At the lodge, you can see this partly Tudor mansion, once the home of the Oglanders, a remarkable local family. Turn right by the lodge and in the wood bear left at first, then turn right uphill to Brading and Nunwell Downs. The clear path leads to a main road. There's a good view from here across to the sea. Cross the road and by the picnic area there is a path down by Adgestone Vineyard - one of a growing number of vineyards in Southern England which are helping to revive fine English wines - to a tarmac lane. Bear right then immediately left, following this lane to Brading. On the right is a well-preserved Roman villa. Evidently the Romans enjoyed the Isle of Vectis as much as modern Britons and this is might be described as an early example of a retirement home.

You also pass Morton Manor, a country house and garden open to the public during the summer months. Bear right and proceed to the traffic lights. Cross over the road and beyond the railway track is a path on the left to Brading Station. It crosses the railway again, and passes by a number of houses towards the station entrance.

If you are visiting Brading, follow the main road mentioned earlier into the village centre. There are shops and pubs as well as attractions like the Lilliput and Wax Museums and Brading Old Town Hall.

Continuing from the station entrance, bear right before the row of houses and walk beyond the garages before turning right to cross the tracks. Go through the kissing gate and the path is to the left across this reclaimed land to the bridge across the River Yar. This was at one time the sea edge and Brading had its own quay. The marshes lower down provide an interesting habitat for wildfowl.

This is the Bembridge Trail and the path from here onwards is clearly marked to Bembridge Windmill. Go over this and the next sluice bridge and the track bears left at the bottom of Centurion's Hill. Proceed through the wood keeping to left turning paths (ignore paths leading off to the right). Eventually you come out into a very large field usually planted with a cereal crop. Bear diagonally right across it. The tracks indicate that some people follow the perimeter of the field to the gate rather than on the right of way.

Bembridge Windmill

Your immediate destination, Bembridge Mill can be seen clearly now. Proceed across two meadows and the northern edge of Bembridge Airfield before reaching the causeway which curves around to a stile. Your way is slightly to the left up the hill and at the top of the field turn right towards the windmill, with the hedge and fence on the left. Cross the stile then turn right along the track to the windmill. Completed in about 1700, much of the original wooden machinery remaining in the mill is typical of that period. It was used to produce flour, meal and cattle feed. It ceased to be used commercially just before the outbreak of the First World War.

At the junction by the mill, turn right down to the wood; shortly after entering it bear left, cross the road and continue uphill by the camp site. At the road, bear right then left onto a lane signed to Whitecliff Bay Holiday Centre. Opposite the camp gift shop, bear right up the concrete road between the chalets towards the coast. You join the coastal path. Turn right and follow this up towards the Yarborough Obelisk named in memory of the first Earl of that name. The path passes just beneath the monument to meet the tarmac road. Bear right and in a short distance left again. The coastal walk into Sandown is very well-defined and easy to follow. There are marvellous views from along it across Sandown Bay.

Sandown

Sandown and its neighbour Shanklin became very fashionable in the last
century with a host of celebrated figures visiting, or staying in the area -
Lewis Carroll, Garrick, Keats, Longfellow and even Continental Royalty.
There was a regular steamer service to Cherbourg, Portsmouth and
Bournemouth from the Pier, which is itself quite a feature, being fully
875 feet long. There are lovely bathing beaches, cafes and all the usual
seaside attractions. The coastal path leads down to the seafront by the
zoo. It's a short walk to the station from the centre of town.

Sandown Bay

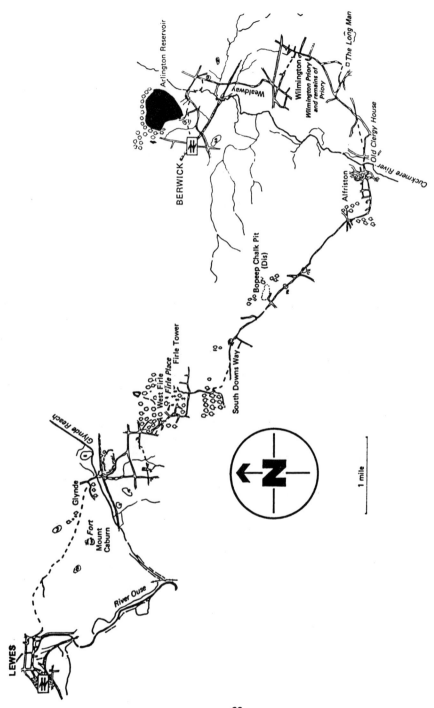

WALK THREE: Along the South Downs

Landranger Maps: Sheets 198, 199

Pathfinder: Sheet TQ 40/50

Starting Station: Berwick

Finishing Station: Lewes

Distance: 15 miles(24 km)

Time Required: 6 hours

Grade: Moderate.

Possible Cut-Off Point: Bopeep Picnic Site 7 miles (12km) with a walk along lanes to Berwick Station. The walk can also be finished at Glynde Railway Station 12 miles (19 km)

Terrain: A ramble across fields and pasture along the South Downs with gentle climbs.

Refreshment and Accommodation: Facilities at Lewes, Eastbourne and to a lesser extent Alfriston on route.There are youth hostels at the latter two locations.

Tourist Information: 3 Cornfield Terrace, Eastbourne (0323) 27474/21333 *or* 32 High Street, Lewes (0273) 471600

THE RAIL JOURNEY

The line from London to Hastings via Lewes and Eastbourne is a busy one through heavily populated areas and it's only towards Haywards Heath that the countryside begins to open up. This is a gentle landscape

23

denuded of much of its natural mixed woodland, but nevertheless offering an appealing prospect for the walker. In just over the hour from Victoria, you are in Lewes, the county town of East Sussex, where it is more than likely that you'll need to change trains for Berwick. Lewes is a handsome Victorian station full of interest, so a 20 minute break to look around it is no hardship. It is also the junction for trains to Newhaven and Seaford.

Alfriston

Berwick is on the Brighton to Eastbourne line which was originally constructed by the Brighton, Lewes and Hastings Railway in 1846. The fast local train covers the 7 mile direct journey from Lewes in 12 minutes. The walk back takes a little longer, but is worth every minute.

THE WALK

Once out of Berwick station, cross the road and bear left. Almost immediately, turn right between the shop and the petrol station over a stile, the path being signposted to Arlington Reservoir. Berwick is not renowned for much, but there was once one celebrated organisation based in the village known as "The Sparrow and Rat Club" whose Chairman and also President was the local Parson. The main aim of the Club was to kill as many sparrows and rats as possible to keep their numbers down !

Your way continues ahead, slightly left to another stile. Aim again left of the electricity poles towards two stiles and a sleeper over the brook. Follow the fence on your right over the brow, then right and left down to the tarmac lane. There are good views of Arlington Reservoir on this section. Bear left, then in a very short distance right again over a stile into an area of wet ground, across stiles by the reed fringed pond, and on to another tarmac lane. Bear left and walk to the far end of the bridge over the Cuckmere River.

The Wealdway

For some miles this walk follows the path known as the Wealdway, a long distance footpath from Gravesend to Eastbourne, to 'The Long Man' south of Wilmington Village. The path is well-defined in most places and clearly waymarked. Once across the bridge turn right, go over the stile into the pasture scented by the waft of stinking hellebore from the river banks. Before the next hedge, bear left and follow the path up to a stile. Go over it and turn right, once again keeping company with the hedge on the right, a hedge decorated in autumn with sloes, hips and haws. The South Downs are ahead of you; The Long Man, and Alfriston's church spire not far away. Cross the railway line with extreme care, then bear slightly left to a stile, alongside an intriguing marshy remnant then onwards along the field boundary to the main A27 road. Cross over, again with care, into Milton Street and shortly on the left is a path signed to Wilmington, by a garden then over a stile. Maintain your progress along this clearly defined path to the village, where you make a turn right at the tarmac lane.

The Long Man

This somewhat virile figure has intrigued historians and archaeologists through the ages. Before you come to the full frontal, it is perhaps worth mentioning about the Priory tucked away in this exceedingly neat village. Its remains have partly been incorporated into a museum featuring agricultural implements of a past age. There's also a seat, dedicated to a local author, where you can rest, overlooking the Long Man on the northern slopes of Windover Hill.

Is he an Iron Age Fertility Symbol or a latter day folly? The great carving on the chalk hillside still remains a mystery, though informed opinion tends towards the former. What is factual is that this huge outline of a human with staff in each hand is 227 feet (73 metres) high.

Your path continues to the left, almost up to the foot of the figure , then follows a route to the right. There are fine views from here to the Weald in the north and soon towards Alfriston in the west. For anyone not used to chalklands the broad, white path will seem quite unusual. Bear right at the crossroads leading down to a tarmac road, then left for a short distance and as the road curves to the right take the path on the right, over the stile and across another stile towards Alfriston church. The views, in clear weather, are quite magnificent.

Continue down the well-defined path to a nasty bend by a beautifully restored house, then bear almost immediately left over a distinguished white footbridge into the village.

Alfriston

Apart from the endless stream of coaches along its main street, this village is idyllic and a good place for a short break. Most of the pubs welcome walkers if you are prepared to take muddy boots off. The village clearly caters for tourists, but nevertheless manages to retain much of its original charm. Not so in past centuries, when the village had a reputation for smuggling. The Alfriston Smugglers were notorious, but the ring collapsed when the leader was sentenced to seven years transportation to Australia, ironically for sheep stealing. The Old Clergy House, next to the village green, dates from the 14th century. It was also the very first property to be acquired by the National Trust in 1896.

South Downs Way

In the village bear, left and proceed as far as The Wingrove where you bear right. Then turn left into The King's Ride (signed on a concrete marker "South Downs Way") soon rising up to the Downs along a wide track surrounded by bushes. Avoid paths to the left and right, following the Way upwards, curving right at first then leading to a walkers' crossroads. Continue ahead along the well-defined path. Ahead of you is a superb landscape, carefully ploughed fields, the sea and the Sussex Weald to the north. The path leads to a kissing gate, then continues along the scarp to a picnic area near Bopeep Chalk Pit. This is a possible cut-off point for anyone needing to end the walk early. To do so, bear right down the tarmac lane, beyond Bopeep Farm to the main A27 road. Cross over and continue along Common Lane back to Berwick village. Turn left for the station.

For Glynde and Lewes, go through two sets of gates and continue along the South Downs Way to Firle Beacon (Trig Point on right). On your left is a long barrow and in the distance Newhaven Harbour. Go through the gate and then take the less distinct path to the right following the contours down to the wood's edge. You can see in the foreground Firle Place, a building dating back to Tudor times, though with later modifications. Go through the gate, continue down to the track before bearing left.

Firle and Glynde

This brings you to Firle village which looks almost medieval in layout and has a traditional pub, The Ram to match. At the first junction, turn right and at the second, left, onto a signposted track. The path curves to the left of a barn and follows the remains of a hedge to a gate. In the next field, keep to the hedge on your left, go over the stile and continue ahead onto the farm drive. At the tarmac lane bear right, cross over the A27 and continue ahead to Glynde village. The Trevor Arms, serving food and a commendable pint of Harveys, is on the left before the railway station. If you get waylaid here, there's an hourly service home but it would be a pity to miss the very fine final section of the walk to Lewes.

Up the road a little way is the world famous Glyndebourne Opera House. The house you see today was substantially rebuilt in Tudor style in the last century. Closer, a matter of metres on the right, is the entrance to Glynde Place, a dignified house built in the 16th century.

Lewes

Once a Saxon stronghold, taken over with some force by the Normans soon after the Battle of Hastings, Lewes has always been a strategic defensive site, as well as an important centre for communications for the region. The Castle testifies to this. It is a mighty structure, perched above the High Street, and offering commanding views of the Downs and, in the distance, the sea. It was founded by William de Warenne, a henchman of William the Conqueror. Loyal to Henry III, its troops withstood an assault by Simon de Montfort and other barons in 1264, but subsequent victory by de Montfort in the Battle of Lewes is judged to be the very first step towards Parliamentary Democracy in Britain. Another link with democratic rights is the fact that the writer Tom Paine, author of the influential pamphlet "The Rights of Man", published in 1791, lived and worked here as a customs officer between 1768 to 1774 before going to America to support the American and later the French Revolutions.

The Castle is open to the public and a combined ticket also gives access to the Lewes Living History Pavilion. Here you'll find a model of the town as it would have been a hundred years ago. There's also a "Son-et-Lumiere" programme depicting the history of Lewes, using the model to highlight key developments.

The town itself is full of architectural splendours with many Georgian houses and shops, made even more fascinating because of the tiny passages and narrow lanes between them known as "Twittens", most probably dating from earlier times. There are two very good museums, one in Barbican House and the other in Anne of Cleeves' House, given to Anne when Henry VIII divorced her (his fourth wife) in 1540. And if you enjoy a glass of old English beer before the train home, there are a number of hostelries in Lewes, many of them serving the excellent products of traditional brewers Harvey and Son, established in 1790.

Pass Glynde Station and take the next turn left by the Post Office and then bear right on to the well trodden-path, mid field. Continue ahead, crossing a stile, to the brow of the hill. Mount Caburn, an Iron Age hill fort can be seen on the left here. Go over another stile, then the path descends mid field once again towards a dry valley. Go left over the stile, down the valley bottom, to another stile next to a Dew pond. Go over this and walk up to yet another stile, the path now climbing upwards across the field. Over another stile and left once again rising to a bluff and on to a golf course. From here there's a superb view of Lewes. Pass by the club house and the lane leads down to the town centre. The elegance of the old town comes as a bit of a culture shock after all those lonely miles on the hills.

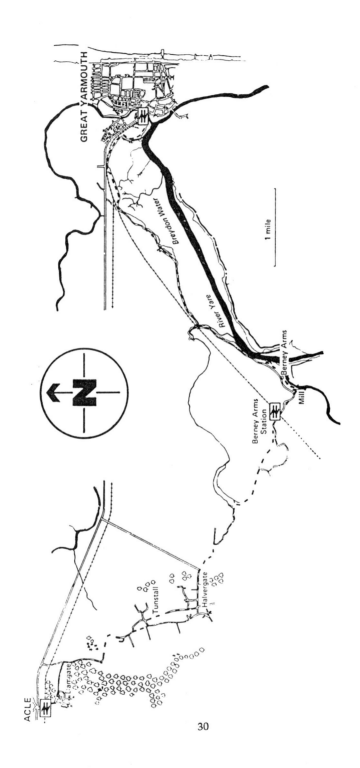

GREAT YARMOUTH

Breydon Water

River Yare

Berney Arms

Berney Arms
Station

Mill

1 mile

N

Tunstall

Halvergate

Larrgate

ACLE

WALK FOUR: Norfolk Broadlands

Landranger Map: Sheet 134

Pathfinder Map: Sheet TG 40/50

Starting Station: Acle

Finishing Station: Great Yarmouth

Distance: 11 miles (17.5km)

Time: 5 hours

Grade: Easy.

Possible Cut-Off Point: Berney Arms halt. 6 miles (10 km).

Terrain: Walking along gently undulating tracks, flat marshland and a riverside path.

Refreshment and Accommodation: Plentiful supply at Norwich or Great Yarmouth including a youth hostel at both locations. More limited at Acle.

Tourist Information: South Quay, Great Yarmouth (0493) 846345/846344 *or* Goal Street, Norwich (0603) 666071

THE RAIL JOURNEY

The more romantic route to Norwich is by way of Ely, with its hauntingly beautiful cathedral dominating the skyline and on to the market town of Thetford. The journey out via Ipswich is far faster, but less inspiring. Either way you soon begin to sense a feeling of isolation, for Norfolk is a vast agrarian county with a sparse population, something you'll not fail to note on this walk.

All of the existing railways converge on Norwich, the lines from Lowestoft and Sheringham, as well as the Birmingham and London links, making it a busy terminus. Norwich itself is very much the capital city of East Anglia. It has been a market centre for well over a thousand years and the Normans consolidated it as a strategic settlement by building a castle and cathedral, the latter being founded in 1096. The Norwich Castle Museum is also well worth a visit if time permits. But the city is full of interesting attractions. One favourite is the Mustard Shop which houses a small museum and also dispenses traditional condiments to suit your taste - savorona, tarragon or something sharper should you prefer.

Berney Arms Windmill

The local trains out of Norwich to Great Yarmouth, a town more commonly referred to as Yarmouth, serve a number of suburban and rural communities. The 10 mile journey to Acle takes about twenty minutes. Acle owes its existence as a bridging point across the River Bure. Lying on higher ground, it has established itself as a small market town renowned for its pig market. It is not really a centre of boating activity, although it is firmly in "The Broads". This series of channels, rivers and lakes, many of them created by man as a result of extraction of peat, attracts thousands of visitors every summer, and its natural beauty, together with the threat caused by heavy recreational use and agricultural changes, have now persuaded the government to consider the area as a National Park.

Many visitors, of course, simply spend their time cruising up and down in motor powered boats, a phenomenon you'll be able to observe on the latter stages of the walk. That's why, if you want to enjoy The Broads at their best, come out of season.

THE WALK

As the road veers away to the left at the station entrance, bear right down a track to the B1140, go right under the bridge then cross over to take the first left turning just before the telephone kiosk, signed to Damgate Marshes. Beyond the sewage works, this is crossed by another track. Bear right here following the ditch until it curves to the right. Continue ahead to the barn where the path bends to the left. Follow this until it meets another track where you turn right passing by Staithe Farm. This is The Weaver's Way footpath route from Cromer to Stalham. It is pleasing to see that hedges have been replanted here to break up the monotony of the beet and corn belt. As the lane winds around to the left, continue ahead on the clear path up to the little used church at Tunstall hamlet. This is an area of ancient churches, marvellous landmarks in otherwise flat terrain. Bear left on the lane and then right by the telephone kiosk onto a direct path to Halvergate village, the largest settlement on the route. At the tarmac lane turn left. Pass by the Red Lion Inn, unless temptation overcomes you, and follow this road until it bends sharply left.

Halvergate Marshes

These marshes make up the largest area of grazing wetlands of this nature in the country, best appreciated when there is a light swirling mist and the local cows are bellowing like elephants. Some of the old windpumps can be seen in the distance, a reminder of the time when the marshes were drained entirely by natural power. The walk through to the Berney Arms takes you across numerous ditches; an opportunity to see at fairly close quarters a number of visiting birds, including waders.

At the bend, bear right and beyond the barn, at the junction of gates, bear right again for the Berney Arms path, reopened to the public in 1985. Follow this to the right of the windmill, go right over the ditch, then the path leads round to the next bridge. Cross over and bear right along a well worn track, through a barred gate, then taking the path, signposted, slightly left towards the next bridge. Go over it and continue ahead, slightly right, to a barred gate where you must turn left then immediately right into a field where the path lies ahead just to the right of the ditch. The Berney Arms Mill is a landmark now before you. Go through the gateway, bear slightly right to another small wooden bridge, cross over, then turn left along the channel. The path is clearly marked from here to the railway line. Cross over the tracks. This is the Berney Arms Halt, surely the remotest railway station in the East of England, and incidentally one of the lowest in Britain, being just below sea level! If you are finishing the walk here, check your train times before visiting the mill and pub.

The Berney Arms.

The windmill, owned by English Heritage, is one of the finest examples of a working mill remaining in the country. Such mills were used for grinding corn and pumping water but also for other purposes on occasion. The clear path down from the railway comes out at the mill. Bear left and in a short distance is "The Berney Arms", Norfolk's only pub without road access. You can come here either by train, boat or on foot - not by car. It was built originally to serve local workers and passing vessels plying their way up river to Norwich. Closed in 1898 after some unfortunate drowning incidents, it regained its licence in 1953. Most trade comes by boat, but walkers are also made welcome. It is not open during the depths of winter.

The River Yare

The path passes by the pub and now follows the riverside, clearly defined all of the way into Yarmouth. The Yare is a broad river capable of handling sea going vessels up as far as Norwich, but it is usually full of pleasure boats. It is the home of a variety of waterfowl and estuarial birds continually being put to flight by boat activity on the river. As you approach Great Yarmouth, with the railway lines coming close to your route, one path crosses both lines to the left of Breydon Junction with a walk down the A47 to town, but most walkers prefer to follow the estuary path under the new bridge and into the town via the industrial area behind the station.

Great Yarmouth

Great Yarmouth is a popular seaside resort, crowded throughout the season, with two fine piers and miles of golden sand. It is is also an ancient, working port whose harbour walls go back to the 13th century. The town was immortalised by Charles Dickens in "David Copperfield" as well as being the birthplace of Anna Sewell (1820-78), authoress of "Black Beauty" - the 17th century house in Church Plain in which she was born is now a small museum. But Yarmouth has a number of different faces. Sandwiched between the holiday resort and the harbour is an old town with narrow streets, atmospheric passageways and rich character. Give yourself time to explore them if you can, and to visit the Maritime Museum and the Tollhouse, with its 13th century dungeons, said to be the oldest surviving civic building in Britain. There's also a wide choice of facilities to attract the weary traveller even if his or her stay, like David Copperfield's, can be only of a short duration before a journey home.

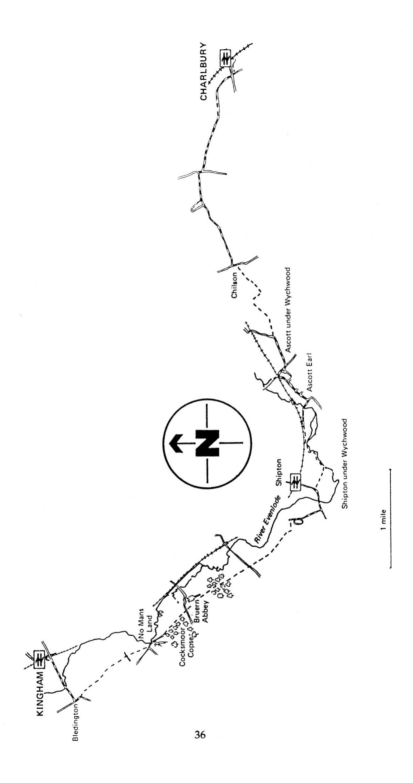

CHARLBURY

Chilson

Ascott under Wychwood

Ascott Earl

Shipton under Wychwood

River Evenlode

Shipton

N

KINGHAM

Bledington

No Mans Land

Cocksmoor Copse

Bruern Abbey

1 mile

WALK FIVE: The Oxfordshire Way

Landranger Map: Sheets 163 & 164

Pathfinder Map: Sheets SP21/31 & SP22/32

Starting Station: Kingham

Finishing Station: Charlbury

Distance: 11 miles (18 Km)

Time Required: 5 hours

Grade: Easy to Moderate

Possible Cut-Off Point: Shipton under Wychwood, 6 miles (10.5km).

Terrain: Very gentle countryside along well-defined field paths in most places.

Refreshment and Accommodation: Plentiful supply in Oxford, Evesham and Worcester. Also limited supply in Moreton-in-Marsh, Kingham, Charlbury and the villages on route. The village pubs are delightful. Youth hostels at Charlbury and Oxford.

Tourist Information: High Street, Moreton-in-Marsh(0608) 50881 *or* St Aldates, Oxford (0865) 726871.

THE RAIL JOURNEY

Kingham is on the line now known as the Cotswold and Malvern, or the Cotswolds Line for short. In recent years, this section of the rail network has been enjoying something of a renaissance including the re-opening of stations such as Honeybourne. There is a strong community interest in the line and this is reflected in the work of the Cotswold Line Association which helps British Rail get its publicity distributed throughout the area and to maintain the excellent condition of the railway stations, including the unmanned halts.

This line has an interesting history. The Oxford, Worcester and Wolverhampton Railway as it was known, opened in June 1853 after several years of wrangling. There was a preview for the Directors and VIPs in May with a champagne lunch in Evesham, followed by a formal opening in June (without champagne) for passengers. The line has always been a reasonably important link, but at one stage it looked destined for obscurity with the withdrawal of through trains to Paddington. Campaigning by local activists had brought a positive response from British Rail resulting in the kind of co-operation with local community interests that is helping the line to flourish through the late 1980s.

On The Oxforshire Way

Whether you travel to Kingham by way of Oxford or Worcester, the views will be pleasant. Via Worcester you pass Evesham, a market town situated on the banks of the River Avon, with a number of interesting buildings in the central area. Moreton-in-Marsh is also another delightful market town, rich in Cotswold character. From the other direction, Oxford itself is the major attraction, being one of most famous seats of learning and scholarship in the Western World. The colleges, the gardens and museums make Oxford an fascinating place to visit. But it takes the train only 10 minutes to get you out into West Oxfordshire, a placid landscape with a patchwork of fields and clustered villages, distinctive in their mellow Cotswold stone. It also has its fair share of country houses and parkland. Not far away from Handborough station is Blenheim Palace, an 18th Baroque palace, designed by the great English architect and playwright Vanbrugh, birthplace of Winston Churchill and the home of the present (11th) Duke of Marlborough. Between Finstock and Charlbury, Cornbury House and Deer Park is on your left. The line follows the Evenlode valley through to Kingham, once a junction for trains to Chipping Norton and Cheltenham via Bourton-on-the-Water.

THE WALK

From Kingham Station approach, bear right towards Bledington village on the path alongside the B4450. At the first junction, turn left signed to Foscot and Idbury. As the road bends to the right, go through a barred gate, then through another barred gate before bearing right keeping by the wire fence and hedge until you reach a large isolated oak tree. The path is waymarked to the left and then follows a drainage channel almost to the river where it forks off at right angles up to a woodland nature reserve. Take the path immediately to your left through the wood to a bridle gate leading into pasture. Continue ahead keeping Cocksmoor Copse to your right as far as the tarmac lane. Cross over into the parkland adjacent to Bruern Abbey, a fine country house with interesting gardens.

This is one of the features of "The Oxfordshire Way"; not a mile passes by without there being a change of scenery, from arable land to parkland, through villages that have stood since Domesday times, by stretches of delightful riverside. The Way was created very much as a result of countryside user groups planning the route and campaigning for footpath improvements over a long period. As you will have probably noticed, much of the route is waymarked and being well used.

At first bear slightly left, then curve to the right towards the stile, mid field, continuing ahead to a bridle gate. Follow the shallow channel between Bruern Wood and Meadow Copse. At the far end the path leads off to the left, and goes through a bridle gate. Keep the hedge to your right until the next bridle gate, which seems to guide you through a private racecourse. Cross the lane and continue ahead on the well-defined path over four stiles towards the spire of Shipton church.

Wychwood Forest

The path then sweeps through a field with grubbed hedges, bears off to the left, then bears sharp right onto a muddy track leading to Shipton-Under-Wychwood, once part of a favourite hunting ground for Kings of England. Shipton was one of several villages situated in the Royal Forest of Wychwood, though most of the original woodland has long vanished. The village is to your right, the focal point being the green near to the church. The Red House pub is the nearest refreshment point, but further along the road is the ancient Shaven Crown. Shipton Court is a distinctive Jacobean building dating from 1603.

If you are not going to the village, bear left at the main road towards the railway station which has a handsomely built warehouse nearby. This is a possible cut off point for the walk, but make sure you have checked times carefully as trains stop only infrequently here. Once over the Evenlode, take the second path off to the right beyond the garage. Follow this path to the river bluff along the field boundary. As an alternative, some walkers bear right just beyond the garage to the footbridge over the Evenlode (without crossing) before bearing left along the riverside until the path leads up to the left to meet another path along the field's edge. Either way, follow this path towards the railway and continue ahead to the barred gate leading to a hawthorn sheltered track, then on to the tarmac road. This is Ascott Earl.

The Ascotts

Bear left through the main village of Ascott under Wychwood, passing The Swan tavern on the left. Continue towards the station, bearing right to pass by the Wychwood Arms Hotel. The church is of Norman origin and again there is a fine village green. After the hotel bear left up the High Street to Ascott d'Oyley but as the lane turns left, your way is to the right through the barred gate. The path is not distinct here, but aim diagonally right towards the field corner. Go through the barred gate. The map indicates that you should follow the boundary on your right and at the top of the field bear left. Some walkers however, bear left here and then right at the bottom left hand corner to reach a point where the path bears left between two great old tree stumps - fine specimens they must have been in their prime. Follow this clear path to the hamlet of Chilson.

Turn left, then right, opposite Chilson farm, down a delightful track towards Charlbury. This leads to a tarmac lane, which is followed the short distance to a junction where you bear right then almost immediately left into the fields once again. This well-defined track passes by Walcot Farm eventually coming out on to the B4437. Bear left and the superbly restored railway station, designed by Isambard Kingdom Brunel himself, stands on your right.

The station is kept in an immaculate condition by the railway staff, showing the sort of commitment and enthusiasm to a country railway you'll find all along the line. Mr Brunel would surely have approved.

Charlbury

If you have time, check your train time before wandering into Charlbury, whose lovely name means "town of the free men". Walk up Dyers Hill and right into Market Street. The buildings date mainly from the last two centuries, but the town feels older, probably a reflection of the street layout. On the left is The Corner House dating mainly from the 18th century although, there was a building on the site in earlier times. Next door is the Museum with a waggon dating from 1906 in the forecourt. There are a number of local historical exhibits inside. By now you will have noticed the plentiful supply of hostelries in the town, all of which serve at least bar snacks or something more substantial. Turn right into Church Street, where on the right you'll see The Albright House, named after the Quaker family who occupied it in the last century. The wisteria which adorns the front is magnificient, best enjoyed in its spring glory. Walk down to the church, through the churchyard and into Church Lane to return to Charlbury's splendid station.

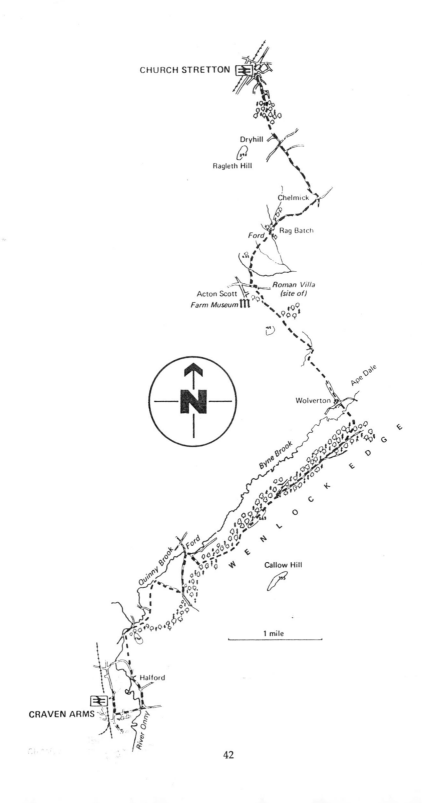

CHURCH STRETTON

Dryhill

Ragleth Hill

Chelmick

Ford

Rag Batch

*Roman Villa
(site of)*

Acton Scott
Farm Museum

Ape Dale

Wolverton

N

Byne Brook

W E N L O C K   E D G E

Callow Hill

Quinny Brook

Ford

1 mile

Halford

CRAVEN ARMS

River Onny

WALK SIX: On Wenlock Edge

Landranger Maps: Sheet 137

Pathfinder Maps: Sheet SO 48/58; Sheet SO 49/59

Starting Station: Craven Arms

Finishing Station: Church Stretton

Distance: 10 Miles (17 Km)

Time required: Five hours

Grade: Moderate.

Possible Cut-Off Point: Wenlock Edge 3 miles (5.5km), with return walk along lanes to Craven Arms.

Terrain: Mainly reasonable paths in gentle landscapes, climbs up to Wenlock Edge and Ragleth hills.

Refreshment and Accommodation: Cafes, shops, pubs, guest house and hotel accommodation at Craven Arms and Church Stretton, more at the latter. Youth hostel at Ludlow with short train ride to Craven Arms.

Tourist Information: Church Street, Church Stretton. (0694) 722535. Not open all year *or* Castle Street, Ludlow. (0584)3857 *or* The Square, Shrewsbury. (0743)50761/52019

THE RAIL JOURNEY

Cardiff to Crewe doesn't sound too exciting for a train journey, but in fact this 138 mile run offers for the most part an enchanting introduction to the Welsh Border Country, the Marches. This area, which for centuries suffered the turbulence of wars and unrest between the Welsh and English, not to mention the activities of Romans, is somewhat quieter now. Evidence of military activity, however, endures. The line of Roman fortresses at Caerleon, Kenchester (near Hereford), Leintwardine (near Ludlow) and Wroxeter (near Shrewsbury) map out the ancient frontier. But medieval castles are equally commonplace; Newport, Abergavenny, Hereford, Ludlow, and Shrewsbury. Some of these can be seen from the train. In more recent and civilised times, these settlements have become market towns, drawing in farmers and their wives from considerable distances to buy and sell produce, stock and other goods. By far the best market to visit is Hereford on a Wednesday. But the train calls at many other towns worth exploring, some as poetic in appearance as their names suggest - Abergavenny for the Black Mountains and Brecon Beacons, Hereford for the beautiful Wye Valley, Leominster (pronounce it "Lemster" to avoid the laughter) and Ludlow - all real Border country towns, before you reach Craven Arms.

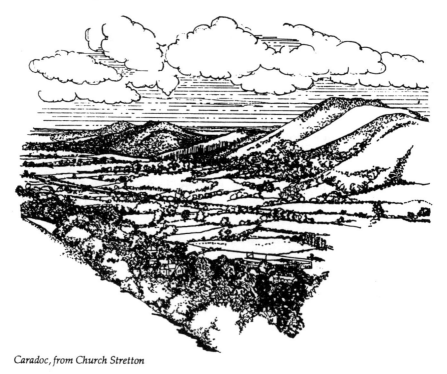

Caradoc, from Church Stretton

If you are travelling from the North, then the journey down from Crewe is just as pleasant, through the rolling plains of Cheshire famous for its dairy products, particularly farmhouse cheeses. Connoisseurs go for the Cheshire or Shropshire Blue sold mainly in the Whitchurch area, but the ordinary white Cheshire Cheese makes a lovely pub ploughman's lunch with a pint of local ale. Talking of which, the next but one station is Wem, a brewery as well as market town. Then on to Shrewsbury, the county town of Shropshire set on the banks of the River Severn, one of England's greatest rivers dedicated by the Romans to the goddess Sabrina and celebrated in English poetry.

Shrewsbury is a fine town with Tudor buildings, busy streets, many of them pedestrianised shopping areas, an abbey and castle amongst its attractions. The train crosses over the Severn, the awesome prison on the left, views of the town to the right, before entering the gently rolling countryside of South Shropshire which soon becomes hillier and more dramatic as the train nears Church Stretton.

Craven Arms owes its existence as a town to the railway. The Shrewsbury and Hereford line, built by one of the most competent railway engineers of the time, Thomas Brassey, was opened in several stages during the early 1850s. The celebrations in the Old Assembly Rooms in Ludlow gives us a clue to the importance of such events, at least gastronomically. The bill of fare included twelve pigeon pies, one large boar's head, twelve ornamental sponge cakes, and eighteen moulds of jelly. Residents of Craven Arms came off particularly well, for there were celebrations for the subsequent opening of branches to Knighton, Bishop's Castle and Much Wenlock. Before the railways came, Craven Arms was nothing more than an inn and a few surrounding dwellings, the meeting place for drovers bringing sheep for sale at autumn time. The railways brought work and Craven Arms became one of the main centres for auctioning sheep. It still is, even though the sheep are no longer brought by rail.

A mile from Craven Arms is Stokesay Castle, a fortified manor house dating from the 13th century, a very unusual survival from this period. It was lived in until 1728, but fortunately it was preserved by the Allcroft family in 1869. There's a great view of the castle from the train, but if you want to take a closer look, it is open throughout the summer months; check times with the Tourist Information office. The railway company thought the castle was important for the station used to be called Craven Arms and Stokesay and had a very long station name board. It's simply Craven Arms now.

THE WALK

Alight at Craven Arms station, bear right at the end of the station approach (cafe opposite is the last for several miles) then go first left. Walk out of the town, over the River Onny and take the first left again. After a short distance the lane bears sharp right; carry straight on past Halford farm and chapel to the cottages. There's a stile on the right with two footpaths signed. Take the path leading off to the left, keeping the hedge to your left. Go over the barred gate and now walk with the broken hawthorn hedge to your right. A stile leads in to a wood. The path soon emerges in a meadow. Continue ahead (with a barn in the distance) and a stile comes into sight on your left. Proceed through the rough wooded area, pass by two houses and go through the barred gate before you. Keep to the left hand side, continuing ahead with the oak tree as a marker. Follow the line of trees towards the footbridge. Do not cross it; bear right to a stile mid field then onwards to the another footbridge leading on to a pleasant lane. Turn left and just before the ford at Strefford, bear right and right again up an old trackway towards the Edge.

Wenlock Edge

The Edge, an impressive limestone ridge, runs south-westwards from Much Wenlock to this point. This is "Shropshire Lad" country, an area made famous by the series of hauntingly melancholy poems of that title by the Edwardian poet, A. E. Housman and what delightful countryside it is. Continue to climb up to the top then bear left along the wooded ridge, a magnificent viewpoint. To your right on Callow Hill you'll notice a tower known as "Flounders' Folly". It was built in 1838 by landowner Benjamin Flounders, some say to create work during a slump, others reckon it was merely built as a boundary marker for large estates. Before long you meet a track. This is the cut-off point for those wishing to return to Craven Arms station. Should you so decide, turn right down the farm track which leads to a tarmac lane. Bear right and right again, to Lower Dinchope, then descend past Ireland Cottage to Halford from where you can retrace your steps to Craven Arms.

If you are continuing to Church Stretton, then bear left at the track, then almost immediately right into thick woodland once more and continue along the well worn path for nearly 2 miles. You come to a stream bed, then almost immediately bear left downwards, the only landmark being Wolverton farm below, which can just be discerned through the trees. Descend to a junction of paths; continue towards the wood's edge where there is an open gateway. Follow the path down to the footbridge and then make your way to the right hand corner of the barn and tarmac lane. If you miss this path down off the Edge don't worry; you eventually come out at a picnic area. Turn left and left again along the tarmac lane to the farm.

Ape Dale

This sleepy valley is characterised by large isolated farms surrounded by fields of wheat and barley. Crossing the tarmac lane, make your way up a track which peters out amid four fields. The Pathfinder map shows the path curving across a very large field ahead to what looks like an area of scrub below. However, most ramblers follow the field's edge down to the line of an old railway where there is access to the trackbed. Go over the broken down fence leading to the bridge over the stream, then bear right over the stile into pasture. Bear leftwards slightly to a point mid-field where two pieces of metal tubing constitute the stile over the fence, then over the drainage ditch by way of the sleeper. Bear right slightly making for the stile, more of a jumble of wood, next to the old tree stump, maintaining a path ahead to another stile often surrounded by nettles. Take care! Continue the short distance ahead, go through the gate, continuing upwards with the fence on your left. Acton Scott Hall is also to your left. Go over the stile in the top left hand corner, bear first right keeping the hedge on your right, then over another stile. There's an access stile directly ahead leading into the car park and picnic area of Acton Scott Working Farm Museum. To your right is the site of a Roman villa.

Acton Scott Working Farm Museum

This excellent museum exhibits life as it was before the introduction of petrol engines. The stock includes horses, cows, sheep, pigs and poultry, many of them being rare breeds. There is also a cafe situated in the old Victorian school house. The museum is open daily from May to the end of October.

From the entrance bear left onto the tarmac lane, then go through the barred gate on the right, opposite the farm. There are fine views of Ragleth Hill and The Long Mynd beyond. Follow the track down to the ford, then climb up with the hedge on your right until the path (with nettles in summer) takes you down to a broken gate that leads to a stream. Cross over and climb up the earth bank to the field's edge. The path is not clear here, but your way is ahead to the brow of the hillock, then left to the barred gate leading to another ford. Climb up Rag Batch, out of the wood and continue ahead keeping the hedge to your right eventually reaching a track leading to the hamlet of Chelmick. Bear left along the tarmac lane, ignoring the first turn right, but bearing right at the next junction. Take the first left turn, signposted, and as the track veers to the left, continue straight ahead over a stile then through a gate onto the open moorland of Ragleth Hill. There's a good view of Caer Caradoc Hill ahead and Hope Bowdler to your right.

Continue down through the wood into the edge of Church Stretton town, going into Poplar Drive, turning left to Ragleth Road, then right into Clive Avenue. Cross the main A49, taking care to avoid heavy traffic, to arrive at Church Stretton railway station entrance ahead. But you'll want to explore this particularily fine town before catching your train.

Church Stretton

Church Stretton is still something of a health resort, with pleasant shops, a Tuesday market (its charter goes back to the time of King John), pubs and cafes, and a superb setting including the great green ridge of Long Mynd, just behind the town. Once known as "Little Switzerland", Church Stretton attracted Victorian and Edwardian gentry seeking both rest and an opportunity to drink the health-giving mineral waters. Rumour has it that some of those waters were brought up daily by train from Llandrindod Wells. But perhaps that ought to be kept a secret!

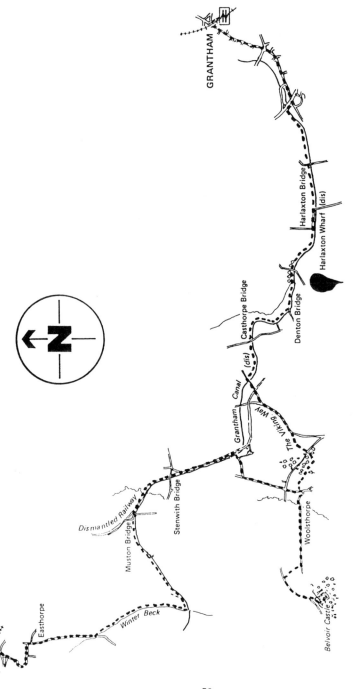

GRANTHAM

Harlaxton Bridge

Harlaxton Wharf (dis)

Casthorpe Bridge

Denton Bridge

Grantham Canal (dis)

The Viking Way

Woolsthorpe

Belvoir Castle

Stenwith Bridge

Dismantled Railway

Muston Bridge

Winter Beck

Easthorpe

BOTTESFORD

N

1 mile

WALK SEVEN: Vale of Belvoir

Landranger Map: Sheet 130

Pathfinder Map: Sheet SK 83/93

Starting Station: Grantham

Finishing Station: Bottesford

Distance: 15 miles (24 km) if Belvoir Castle included, 13 miles (20 km) if not.

Time Required: 6 hours, more if a visit to Belvoir Castle is anticipated.

Grade: Moderate.

Possible Cut-Off Point: There is an afternoon bus from Woolsthorpe to Grantham on Mondays to Saturdays. Contact Tourist Information to check times before travelling.

Terrain: Very gentle and still landscape. Much of the walk is along the towpath of the Grantham Canal.

Refreshment and Accommodation: Cafes, shops, pubs, guest house and hotel accommodation in Grantham. There is also a Youth Hostel.

Tourist Information: The Museum, St Peter's Hill, Grantham.

THE RAIL JOURNEY

Grantham has a guaranteed place in modern British history, being the birthplace of Mrs Margaret Thatcher, Britain's first woman Prime Minister, daughter of a Grantham grocer.

Interestingly enough, Britain's first uniformed policewoman, Edith Smith, also came from Grantham, serving there during the First World War.

Prime Ministers and policewomen apart, there are other reasons to come to the town. Grantham is on the newly electrified East Coast Main Line railway between King's Cross and the North, so is easily accessible from almost anywhere in Britain. It is also the junction for important cross country rail routes to Skegness and Nottingham. The line to Bottesford began life as the Nottingham, Vale of Belvoir and Grantham Railway, but as with so many Victorian railway concerns, was soon taken over by a rival company. Predatory practices among 19th century railway companies make the Stock Exchange of the 1980s seem like the proverbial Vicar's tea party.

Belvoir Castle

This line through the East Midlands used to be extremely busy with freight traffic, including the carriage of iron ore from the Vale of Belvoir itself. Perhaps coal mining in the area, another controversial topic, will bring about the reopening of old lines once again. The Nottingham-Grantham link has also traditionally carried excursion traffic from the industrial Midlands to Skegness, a resort made famous by the LNER fisherman poster with its slogan "Skegness - So Bracing".

Grantham has always been a strategic communication centre, situated by the River Witham under the shoulder of Lincolnshire's limestone Wolds. It was not the railways that first brought commerce, but the Great North Road between London and Scotland, with its constant stream of stage-coaches and carriers' wagons. Many of the inns built to accommodate this trade survive to this day, such as the Angel and Royal, and The George, described so vividly by Dickens in "Nicholas Nickelby".

The town is full of buildings of interest and character to explore before or after the walk, including the 14th century church of St. Wulfram, whose huge tower with its richly decorated spire that climbs 281 feet above the Lincolnshire plain, is a famous landmark. The Museum on St Peter's Hill houses a number of local collections. In Castlegate is Grantham House dating from the 14th century, but with substantial alterations from later periods. It was occupied by the Hall family, a member of which was the first English translator of Homer's "Iliad". But perhaps the most remarkable figure to come from the area was Sir Isaac Newton, the 17th century mathematical genius whose theories of the Laws of Gravity and Motion laid the foundation for the development of the modern sciences of Physics and Astronomy, and for man's understanding of the universe. Born in Woolsthorpe Manor, Colsterworth, near Grantham, he attended the local Grammar School, now King's School, and duly carved his name on a window ledge where it can still be seen. His statue stands by the Guildhall and a new shopping centre has been named after him; one wonders whether he would have approved. But no doubt were he to return as a ghostly presence, he would at least recognise the town on a Saturday when Grantham is filled with a traditional street market.

THE WALK

From Grantham Station entrance, bear left onto Station Road to the roundabout where you should continue straight ahead if you are going to take a look around Grantham town. Otherwise go left under the railway bridge. Follow this road, the Harlaxton Road (A607), for over a mile through an urban area to just beyond the A1 embankment. Take the access path on the right to the Grantham Canal to find peace and quiet. The walk now follows this lovely old canal towpath for several miles.

Grantham Canal

This waterway was opened in 1797 with the aim of linking Grantham to the Trent at Nottingham, a distance of 33 miles, for the carriage of coal, coke, lime, and agricultural products. Reaching its peak of traffic in the late 1830s, the canal soon began to suffer from the competition of the new railways and, as with so many navigations was bought up by the Ambergate, Nottingham, Boston and Eastern Junction Railway as it was longwindedly known. This became the Nottingham, Grantham Railway and Canal Company which in turn leased its entire interests, including the canal, to the Great Northern Railway under whose auspices goods were carried on a regular basis up until and during the First World War. But traffic declined in the inter-war years and in 1936 the London and North Eastern Railway, its subsequent owners, abandoned the canal altogether.

Viking Way through the Vale of Belvoir

The Grantham Canal is a beautiful waterway, teeming with wildlife and much of the credit for this amenity being readily accessible to the walker must go to the local Canal Society. You pass by Harlaxton Bridge, then on to Denton Bridge, with a picnic site, before reaching Casthorpe Bridge. The canal curves to the right and then you'll come across a footbridge spanning it. Cross over and follow the well-defined path to a white gate and the trackbed of the old mineral railway to Harlaxton. Continue ahead with the field boundary on your left up to a green lane. This forms part of "The Viking Way", a long distance path which crosses Lincolnshire, starting at Oakham, in Leicestershire, and finishing at the Humber Bridge.

As the lane bends to the left, go through the gateway into the field, heading slightly right to the field's edge, then left following a direct line down to the tarmac road through an opening in the hedge. Cross over and continue ahead on a path which is waymarked "Jubilee Way" towards a tipping area. Go left over a stile then sharp right, first along the field's edge then directly ahead down the scarp still keeping reasonably close to the wood. There's a marvellous view, the village and church at Woolsthorpe and Belvoir Castle. Look beyond into the Vale, a classic English landscape, each tranquil village marked by a church tower or spire. The Vale is, of course, still famous for its cheesemaking with a number of traditional creameries making that most famous and tasty of English cheeses, the Stilton.

The path descends to the right of the football pitch and leads over a stile behind the hut onto the cricket pitch. Also in classic English fashion, there's also a welcoming pub, The Chequers.

Belvoir Castle

The track comes out on the main street. If you are taking the diversion to the castle bear left then first right up Belvoir Lane. Go over the River Devon and cross the stile on the left. Continue up this path, keeping the hedge to the right until you reach a field gate. Go right here and at the tarmac road bear left. This leads you to the public entrance to Belvoir Castle. The name, Belvoir, meaning beautiful view, couldn't be more apposite. The castle, a building of architectural elegance outside, and dazzling beauty within, is the home of the present Duke and Duchess of Rutland, the tiniest and much lamented of former English counties. It dates back to Norman times, but suffered considerable damage in civil wars and by a very bad fire in 1816. The present building was rebuilt by the Fifth Duchess of Rutland. Inside, there are priceless treasures including tapestries, silks, porcelain, sculpture and paintings by Poussin, Holbein, Rubens and Reynolds and many others. Give yourself plenty of time to enjoy all that the castle has to offer, including its magnificent gardens.

The most pleasant return route to rejoin the walk is to retrace your steps to the Belvoir village.

After your visit, or if you are not visiting the castle, then bear right in the village main street, opposite a greengrocer's shop, and walk up to the crossroads. Cross over to Sedgemoor Road and after a short distance bear right onto a track leading to a pub locally known as "The Dirty Duck". Go over the canal bridge and bear left onto the canal towpath once again. Continue along the towpath for approximately two miles passing under Stenwith and beyond Muston Bridge. Your destination is clearly in sight - the church spire at Bottesford.

Just over a mile after Muston Bridge, as the canal curves to the right and Muston Gorse Farm appears on the opposite bank, you come to Bridge Number 57. Bear right here and then right again across the brook, following it upstream through a succession of fields to a gate leading to a tarmac lane, Castle View Road. Bear right and follow it up to the first junction where you turn left. This winds up to the main A52; avoid turning to the left unless you are planning to have a look around the village. For the railway station, cross over the A52 and continue ahead for a short distance.

Bottesford

Bottesford has an small market place with the remains of an ancient cross, stocks and whipping posts. There are a number of shops and pubs huddled together on the main street. You'll find a path back to the station by way of the churchyard. If you have time, take a few minutes to explore the splendid church, burial place for several of the Lords of Rutland.

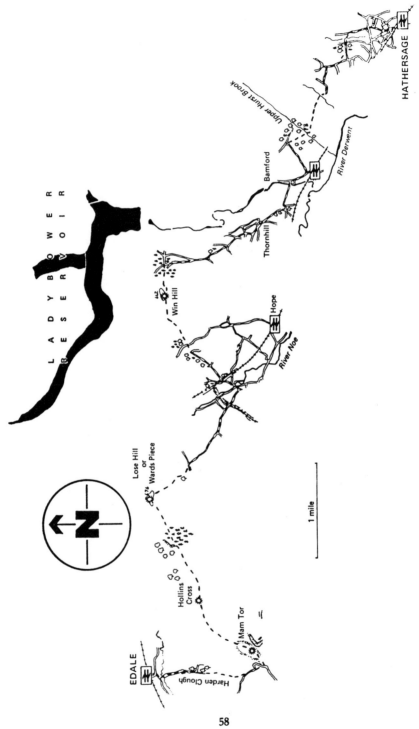

HATHERSAGE

Upper Hurst Brook

Bamford

River Derwent

Thornhill

L A D Y B O W E R
R E S E R V O I R

Win Hill

Hope

River Noe

Lose Hill
or
Wards Piece

1 mile

Hollins
Cross

Mam Tor

EDALE

Harden Clough

N

WALK EIGHT: The Hope Valley

Landranger Map: Sheet 110

Outdoor Leisure Map: Sheet 1 (The Dark Peak)

Pathfinder Map: Sheet SK 28/38

Starting Station: Hathersage

Finishing Station: Edale

Distance: 14 miles (22 km)

Time Required: Allow the best part of a day

Grade: Strenuous. For an easier alternative, end walk at either Bamford or Hope

Possible Cut-off Points: Bamford 2 miles(4 km); Hope 7 miles (11 kms)

Terrain: Easy at first then several steep climbs over high ground. Spectacular views along ridge paths.

Refreshment and Accommodation: There is a good supply of accommodation throughout the Hope Valley and a supply of pubs and to a lesser extent, cafes in the key settlements on route. Youth hostels at Hathersage and Edale.

Tourist Information: Town Hall Extension, Union St, Sheffield (0742) 734671/2. Also, there are *Peak Park Information Centres* at Castleton and Edale.

THE RAIL JOURNEY

The line between Sheffield and Manchester crosses the heart of the Peak District National Park. This is certainly one of Britain's favourite outdoor and walking areas, being only a short rail journey from Manchester and Sheffield and not much further from Merseyside, West Yorkshire or the Midlands.

Even though it runs between such great cities which are not, even in British terms, a long way apart, the train passes through landscape of spectacular wildness and grandeur. Seeing how superbly the landscape has been protected so close to the pressures of urban society, it is little wonder that the Peak District, Britain's first National Park, has won top European awards for its excellence. There are dozens of pretty Peakland villages within easy access to the railway, whilst the landscape is characterised by miles of drystone walling that cross the open moors.

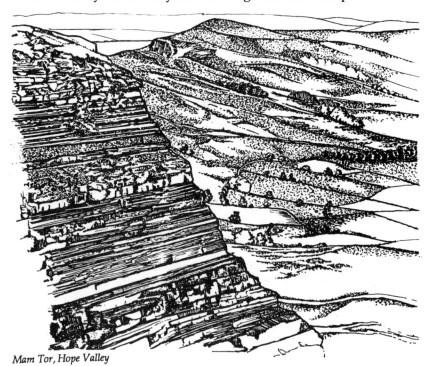

Mam Tor, Hope Valley

Many Peak District villages hold traditional shows and events each year. In particular, the well-dressing ceremonies are very attractive. In the dry limestone areas of the Peak most of the settlements have grown up around wells and for centuries the villages have organised well-dressing festivals of thanksgiving for pure water supplies, usually in late Spring, which have their origin in Pagan worship of wells - as an unfailing source of life-giving water. The art of well-dressing is fascinating and includes the building of surrounds of smoothed clay on which complex pictorial designs are made of natural materials - dried flowers, seeds, bark, and above all flower petals. The decoration is then left at the well for about a week.

The Hope Valley line was developed late in the railway building era. The Dore to Chinley section was only authorised in 1884 and not opened to passengers until a decade afterwards. There was opposition to the line from among local gentry concerned about the implication of opening up the isolated valley of Edale to rail borne visitors. But by the early 20th century, the railways had become established as perhaps the most popular routes out of the cities of Manchester and Sheffield into the Peak District, never more so than in the difficult years of the 1930s, when "hiking" became a national pastime. It is not without significance that Edale was to become the starting point of the 250 mile Pennine Way between the Peak District and Scotland, nor that in the 1960s the then Minister of Transport, Barbara Castle, should refuse permission for the line's closure because of the importance of the line for ramblers into the Peak District - the first time a rail closure had ever been refused for this reason.

Ironically, after the closure of the old Woodhead route first for passengers and then freight, the Hope Valley has become the only line between Sheffield and Manchester, now busy with express trains, freight and local passenger services, increasingly valued as an important tourist route in its own right and means of access to the Peak District National Park.

THE WALK

Alight at Hathersage. It is a fine old village with shops, pubs and even an open air swimming pool. It used to have two tollgates and a smithy and is thought to be the "Morton" in Charlotte Bronte's "Jane Eyre". From the station entrance, bear right and walk a short distance before turning first right into Oddfellows Road. As the road curves to the right, continue ahead to the A625 through a farmyard. Cross the road by the Hathersage Inn and walk along the lane ahead. Shortly on the right, opposite the cricket pitch, is the Shuttleworth Memorial Walk up to the church. In the churchyard lies Little John's Grave, though which Little John is a matter of conjecture. Legend has it that Robin Hood's sturdy friend, on his deathbed, shot an arrow to the spot where he wanted to be buried. It landed near near to the south porch of the church. Thankfully, he was still a reasonable shot, or otherwise he might have been buried almost anywhere.

Edge Views

Just beyond the scout hut, go left through a gap stile and diagonally across to Hood Brook (more associations with Robin ?) cross over the footbridge and then walk directly up the bank following the line of trees to the stile. There are some good views of Stanage and Burbage Edges from here. Then, after a few metres, bear right across a field to another stile leading to a tarmac lane. Bear right and then left at the lane signposted to Bamford. Pass by Thorpe Farm, over a stone stile to the right, and continue slightly left to a stile and then a brook. Cross over and continue ahead to the golf course. You are recommended to keep to the footpath near to the hedge. Regardless of public rights, it is sound advice with all those little white balls flying about. Take special care at the number 12 green and after number 13 bear right down to the footbridge across the Upper Hurst Brook. Bear gently right to the stile just beyond the number 2 green. Turn left along the tree lined Station Road, cross over and go left across the River Derwent. Follow the lane past the Water Authority building, and the path is immediately right across an old railway track bed, then upwards by an ancient sunken track. This is a clear path up to the hamlet of Thornhill where you bear right then left. Pass by the old chapel and then right along Townhead Lane. This soon becomes a well- trodden track and you will see Yorkshire Bridge and Ladybower Reservoir to the right. Ignore the crossing path but shortly afterwards, where the path meets a trackway, continue upwards to the right, eventually levelling out and leading to Winhill plantation.

Once in the wood, take the first path to the left up to Winhill summit (462 metres above sea level). This is a magnificent viewpoint, one of the most famous in the Peak, even though that view includes the chimneys of Bradwell Cement Works, as well as the great expanse of Ladybower Reservoir and the Derwent Valley. There's usually quite a breeze blowing across the top. Ahead of you is Losehill, your next challenge.

Continue ahead to the guidepost, turn left and follow the well-defined and steeply graded route down to Twitchill Farm. Follow the tarmac lane down, under the railway, and to the main Edale road. If you decide to finish the walk at Hope Station (7 miles, 11 kms) here, there is a path off to the left before the bridge over the River Noe, clearly defined, which leads to the A625. Turn left and second left again for Hope Station.

Losehill

To complete the full walk to Edale, cross over the Edale road with the path ahead signed through a gap stile, then over another stile and through a barred gate. Bear right for Losehill summit (signed again) and continue ahead along a well worn path through a series of stiles to cross a footbridge over the cement works rail spur. Go through the gap stile and walk alongside a bungalow. Continue ahead at the crossing of paths and follow the path upwards, Losehill Farm being the landmark to keep your eye on. Keep to the hedge on the right at first, then along a sunken way leading to a stile on the right side of the track. Your immediate target is the barn ahead. Follow the succession of stiles to it and then upwards again to the ladder stile to the right of Losehill Farm. Bear left then right, upwards, with the farm now below you. Keep a steady pace up the steep path to the summit.

Losehill is your second famous Peak District viewpoint, 476 metres high and the start of one of the most famous ridgewalks in England, between Edale and the Hope Valley. A viewfinder at the trig point will enable you to identify other summits and local landmarks.

Bear left to follow the ridge along what was once a packhorse track to Chapel-en-le-Frith, and now is a popular walkers' route. There is a tremendous sense of light and space around you as you follow the path along the ridge over Back Tor with its crags to Hollin Cross.

Hollin Cross, is a celebrated walkers' cross roads, this time on the old 'coffin track' where Edale people used to carry their dead over to the Hope Valley for burial as they had no church of their own. It is now a popular path between Edale and Castleton.

But keep your height on the ridge to ascend the third and highest summit on the walk, Mam Tor (517 metres). Known as "The Shivering Mountain" because of earlier landslips on its unstable shoulders, history has recently repeated itself as the main A625 road between Castleton and Chapel-en-le-Frith has collapsed to a dangerous state and has had to be be closed, despite the efforts of modern highway engineers. The mountain is also famous for its Roman fort on the summit, and is another magnificent viewpoint.

Follow the path down the steps to the road below. Bear right and cut off the first corner by way of a little link path ahead. Back on the road again, bear left and walk the short distance to the stile on the right. The path dips to the left slightly, then descends to the farm below. Follow the tarmac drive down to the road, then turn right, then left for the station and village.

Edale

Whether Edale cherishes its stardom as the starting point of The Pennine Way is a moot point. It is a small village that straggles along a single main street, but you will find two welcoming pubs, a cafe and the excellent Peak National Park Visitor Centre with interpretive displays on local natural history, farming and wildlife. After the triple delights of Win Hill, Lose Hill and Mam Tor, there might be quite a lot to be said for a long, cool, early evening drink outside The Rambler Inn before catching the Hope Valley line train back home. But if you indulge, make sure you don't miss the train!

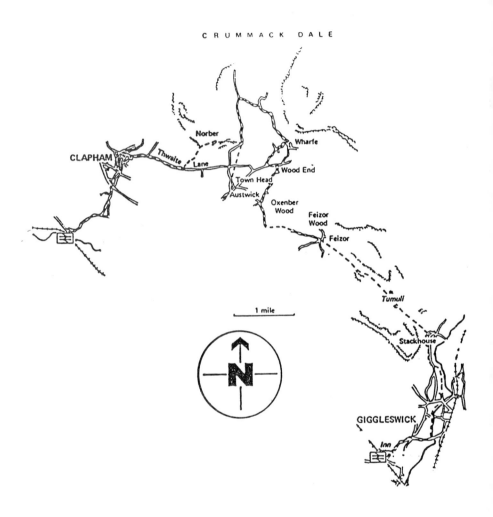

CRUMMACK DALE

Norber

Wharfe

CLAPHAM

Thwaite Lane

Wood End

Town Head

Austwick

Oxenber
Wood

Feizor
Wood

Feizor

1 mile

N

Tumull

Stackhouse

GIGGLESWICK

Inn

WALK NINE: Crummackdale

Landranger Map: Sheet 98

Outdoor Leisure Map: Sheet 2 (Yorkshire Dales Western Area)

Starting Station: Giggleswick

Finishing Station: Clapham

Distance: 10 miles (16 kms)

Time required: $4^1/_2$ hours

Grade: Moderate.

Possible Cut-Off Point: Feizor 4 miles (6. 5km)

Terrain: Field paths across pasture and narrow packhorse tracks. Some muddy stretches after rain and one significant uphill section.

Refreshment and accommodation facilities: Craven Arms Hotel, Giggleswick Station; Settle town (Settle Station on Leeds - Settle - Carlisle line is alternative starting point) with BB, hotels, cafes, shops, Tuesday market; Austwick, mid point on journey has the excellent Gamecock pub, and village shop. Shops, pub, cafes in Clapham; Flying Horseshoe Hotel at Clapham Station.

Tourist Information: Settle Market Place (07292) 3617; Yorkshire Dales National Park Centre, Clapham; office (04685) 419.

THE RAIL JOURNEY

To a very considerable extent the Leeds-Skipton-Morecambe line has been overshadowed by its more dramatic and famous rival, the Leeds-Settle-Carlisle. The two lines separate at Settle Junction, the former skirting the edge of the Yorkshire Dales National Park, the latter ascending the famous "Long Drag" to Ribblehead and Dent.

In fact, this line is the older of the two, having been originally built during the 1840s, some quarter of a century before the Settle-Carlisle, and fully opened between Lancaster, Bentham, Clapham, Hellifield and Skipton, with a branch to Ingleton in 1850 by the North Western Railway Company, sometimes called the "Little North Western" to distinguish it from the larger and more famous London and North Western.

The Ingleton and Lune valley branch to Sedbergh and Tebay closed in the 1950s and, more suprisingly perhaps, the direct line to Lancaster was lifted in the mid 1960s as an early closure in the Beeching era, mainly to remove the need to retain Lancaster's Green Ayre station, leaving the less heavily used Wennington-Carnforth branch as the main route to Lancaster and Morecambe as well as to Furness. Most trains now run down the West Coast main line to serve Lancaster before going on to Morecambe.

The Norber Erratics

It is, in fact, a very beautiful journey over the whole length of the line, particularily west of Skipton where the line curves through the rolling foothills of Craven before skirting the very edge of the Yorkshire Dales National Park, (for a long section the railway actually forms the Park boundary). West of Giggleswick there are spectacular views from both sides of the carriage window - northwards across the limestone scars of the Dales, with the massive summit of Ingleborough itself, a tract of superb scenery exploited by this particular ramble. Southwards the landscape has an equal grandeur, this time formed by the gritstone moors of the Forest of Bowland Area of Outstanding Natural Beauty through which the line, particularly around the Clapham area runs, with Clapham, Bentham and Wennington Stations, providing an excellent means of access to this fine if too little known area. But inevitably, it's the limestone country of the Yorkshire Dales that has to take priority on this walk of surprising contrasts.

THE WALK

Begin at Giggleswick Station, crossing the new Settle by-pass before turning left along the lane towards Settle and Giggleswick. Keep ahead along the lane but look for a large stone built into the wall on the right - this is the Plague Stone where, according to local tradition, during the 16th and 17th century Plagues, villagers were not allowed to pass, leaving money left in lime-water or vinegar in a hollow on the stone for essential purchases. Continue to the cross roads to go directly ahead to the first suburban houses of Settle town.

Along the Ribble Way

Soon past Sandholme Close, part of a new housing estate on the left, look for a little tarmac alleyway between the houses, signed with the little blue Ribble Way sign. Take this, which cuts back into Sandholme Close, but then keep directly ahead to a continuation of the path at the side of the garden which leads through a stile to the River Ribble. Follow the riverside path now behind Settle town. If you want to explore Settle itself, cross over the new Memorial Bridge by Queen's Rock which leads to the town centre. Otherwise, keep ahead to the main road bridge carrying the A65 over the Ribble alongside Settle High School. (Walkers coming from Settle Station or Settle town should join the route here).

Cross with care (this is a blind corner and traffic travels too fast). Follow the enclosed, signposted path directly ahead which winds around the school playing field before reaching a stile and a field path which cuts alongside the river, going through more stiles and a lovely elevated section above the river. This is an area rich in industrial history with several water driven mills dating back to the 18th century still surviving between Settle and Langcliffe.

The path now reaches the lane from Giggleswick. Cross directly ahead, but take the stile directly opposite which leads to a path parallel to the road and behind the wall. Ahead is the hamlet of Stackhouses, enclosed in an area of woodland. Keep left around the outside of the wall ahead, behind Stackhouses, entering scattered woodland and a faint track. Soon you reach a signpost, where the footpath, to Feizor, branches off left, at right angles, directly up the hillside. This is the first and only steep climb on the walk. Head for the right hand of the two wooden step stiles you eventually see in the wall above. From here there are quite superb views back across Ribblesdale with the massive form of Pen y Ghent, one of Yorkshire's celebrated Three Peaks, now dominating the valley behind you, with Fountains Fell beyond.

An Iron Age Barrow

Continue across open pasture. A gate and stile now mark the line of the path ahead. Cross, following the line of a green track which zigzags up, but leave it to bear right towards the wall corner beyond which there is gateway. Go through here, alongside a wall, but after 50 metres or so a low mound of stones on the left marks an Iron Age tumulus or burial site. A complete human skeleton was found buried here last century.

Return to the path and follow the wall on the right. The path soon passes through a gate in the wall to the other side, and sharp left through a second gate. Keep the same direction, now across rough pasture. There are fine views westwards now to Austwick, Wharfe Wood and to the impressive flat-topped shape of Ingleborough itself, at 2373 feet (723 metres) the second highest of the Three Peaks. Go through another gate by a small sheep fold, then follow the path down pasture, balding to limestone pavement, to a further gate ahead and the track into Feizor.

Feizor and its Ancient Packhorse Road

This attractive hamlet was once the site of a monastic grange on the important cross-Pennine packhorse trade route between Lancaster and York, well before the newer turnpike road (now the A65 Leeds-Kendal road) was built for wheeled vehicles.

You can continue directly ahead along a fieldpath opposite the gate that leads into the lane, marked by a line of stiles, and this is a recommended route during or after after wet weather when the ancient bridleway is flooded. But those with a sense of history will want to turn left for a few metres before taking the bridleway - Hale Lane - which soon becomes a narrow packhorse way, winding between walls. The path turns northwards beyond Meldings Barn, below Oxenber Wood, where the fieldpath from Feizor rejoins it. Keep ahead to the cross-roads of tracks where your way is to the right, along Wood Lane. Avoid the next junction right, keeping ahead to join the Austwick-Helwith Bridge road. Go left here for about 200 metres, but turn right almost opposite Silloth House along a lovely little path alongside Austwick Beck to cross Dam House Bridge into the hamlet of Wharfe.

Wharfe - a hidden village

Wharfe is a jewel. Virtually a hidden village, it has a number of fascinating cottages and farms, of which at least one, though it has an 18th century datestone, betrays its Tudor origins with a huge, outside chimney stack. Keep ahead through the village, but soon after the junction with the main lane, right, turn left up a narrow way which seems to climb up round the back of the houses, going in front of a cottage. Keep ahead to a junction to another medieval packhorse way, left, climbing up from the village over the shoulder of Crummackdale.

Into Crummackdale

This enclosed way, White Stone Lane, eventually descends to a junction - keep left here to a ford over Austwick Beck with twin footbridges - one a single slab clapper bridge of ancient design. This is an ideal picnic spot, sheltered from any cold winds. This whole little area is of quite extraordinary geological interest, with, close to the spectacular limestone crags, ancient, dark Ordovician slates making their presence felt in craggy outcrops and knolls, a landscape more typical of the southern Lake District than the Dales.

Continue along the track for 100 metres or so, but look for a stile in the wall, left. Cross here, and climb the fieldpath across the pasture behind, to the summit of the knoll, where you'll find a step stile. Keep ahead, down the hillside, bearing slightly right to locate further stiles in the wall ahead on the access road to Southerthwaite Farm. Another stile leads into the lane, right. For anyone wanting to visit Austwick with its welcoming pub don't go into the lane, but keep ahead to find the stile in the corner of the next field, slightly to the left, following the line of stiles to cross the lane to Slaindale and a partially enclosed way which emerges at Town Head. Keep ahead to the main street into Austwick village. Keep right for the Game Cock Inn.

The Norber Erratics - a geological time machine

If you've gone into Austwick, return the same way to the stile into the lane near Southerthwaite. The walk continues across the lane to the next stile which leads to the path below Nappa Scar, a superb little path offering magnificent views southwards across the Forest of Bowland and, at the Scar itself, a fine example of a geological unconformity, as the massive limestone cliff, together with conglomerate - a kind of geological concrete - rests on a base of Ordovician slate. But more spectacular things are in store. Go through the gap behind the scar to a step stile over the wall, then bear right up the steep hillside onto the back of Norber itself. You will find yourself in a boulder field, filled with ancient, great green lichen-covered rocks of the Silurian era, carried down here by the glaciers of the last Ice Age some 12,000 years ago, looking for the world like giant fossilised iguanas, dumped here as if the ice had only just melted - which in geological terms, of course, it only just has.

These "Norber Erratics" as they are known, are some of the most spectacular geological features of the Yorkshire Dales National Park, particularily impressive where newer limestone rocks sheltered from the frosts and rains have remained as pedestals on which the giants are precariously perched.

Return to the shallow gulley below where a signpost marks the line of path, which goes along the wallside, over a stile, and diagonally across a large open field to a step stile ahead. Note on the right the remains of fieldwalls forming a circular shape, the site of Thwaite Tarn, a glacial lake drained early last century.

Thwaite Lane and Clapham

Turn right when you reach the lane. Easy walking now, along this elevated track, Thwaite Lane, once part of the main road from Leeds to Kendal. There are good views from each side, right across to Robin Proctor's Scar, left across the Wenning Valley to Bowland. Soon past a junction, the track descends quite steeply, going under tunnels built to keep the once busy highway out of the grounds of Ingleborough Hall. Ingleborough Hall was the ancestral home of the Farrer family, Lords of the Manor of Clapham and much of Ingleborough, a noted family of scientists and philanthopists, the most famous of whom being Reginald Farrer, 1880-1920, the great botanist and plant collector, who did much to popularise rock gardening in the British Isles. Ingleborough Hall is now an outdoor education centre.

The tunnels emerge at Clapham's lovely and rather unusual Regency Church (the tower is medieval). The village itself has great character, mainly 18th and 19th century houses and cottages on either side of a central, wooded stream, Clapham Beck, with pretty bridges and beckside paths and an old market cross. There are also cafes, pubs, loos, and the National Park Information Centre. Brookside House Cafe, on the road to the station, particularily welcomes ramblers - and has overnight accommodation for anyone missing the train.

Allow a good half hour for the 1¹/₄ mile walk along the lane to the station. Sadly, most of the original 1840s buildings at the station have been recently demolished owing to dry rot, but there is a shelter on the eastbound platform and, if you've timed it well, the Flying Horseshoe. But make sure, particularily if you are lucky enough to enjoy a fine late afternoon, you enjoy the really quite stunning views of the Bowland Fells from the platform, before the little diesel "Pacer" train comes round the curve to whisk you home.

Piked Howes

Crabtree Brow

Garburn Pass

Garburn Road

Kentmere Hall

Garburn
Nook

Nook
Kentmere

Stunfell Howe

Trout Beck

Backstone Barrow

Whiteside End

River Kent

Park Beck

Dubbs Beck

Dubbs
Reservoir

Works

Sawmill
Cottage

Croft
Head

Millrigg Knott

Ullthwaite Bridge

Browfoot

Moor Howe

Near Orrest

N

High Knott

Goose
Howe

Orrest
Head

Scroggs
Bridge

Elleray
Bank

1 mile

WINDERMERE

STAVELEY

WALK TEN: Kentmere and the Garburn Pass

Landranger Maps: Sheets 97, 90

Outdoor Leisure Map: Sheet 7 English Lakes (South East)

Starting Station: Staveley

Finishing Station: Windermere

Distance: 9 miles (14.5kms)

Time required: 4 hours

Grade: Moderate.

Possible Cut-Off Point: Kentmere $3^1/_2$ miles (5.5km)

Terrain: Lane, tracks, field and woodland paths. Two short but significant climbs, but generally easy walking on clearly defined paths.

Refreshment and accommodation facilities: Staveley has an inn, shops, a cafe. Windermere is extremely well supplied with everything - pubs, cafes, hotels, bed and breakfast facilities, shops. Youth Hostel in Kendal.

Easy or bad weather alternative: Level walking to Kentmere - return same route or along the lane.

Tourist Information: Town Hall, Kendal (0539) 27578 *or* The Gateway Centre, Windermere (09662) 6499

Not many railway lines can boast to have provoked the wrath of a Poet Laureate, but the Kendal-Windermere Railway caused Wordsworth himself to raise his pen in white-hot fury:

"Is then no nook of English ground secure from rash assault?"

begins his quite unmemorable sonnet when, in 1844 the old man joined the objectors to a proposed railway to Ambleside. "Hear YE that whistle?", he continues in another finger-wagging sonnet urging the mountains to look on the railway building with suitable disdain.

It seems impossible to imagine that any threat to the landscape could come from the little branch line, now single track, which blends so unobtrusively into the landscape. Ironically, if Wordsworth was alive and writing now, he would undoubtedly be in the forefront of the railway preservation movement and objecting to the motor car. And he would have a point. The nearby A591, widened in many places, makes a far greater impact on the Lakeland landscape.

But to an extent, the protesters were successful. The line's promoters soon gave up any attempt to put down metal lines into the heart of the old lion's den, at Ambleside, but terminated the railway at Applethwaite, an obscure hamlet above Bowness, which the railway company had the wit to rename Windermere and thereby establish the identity of the new town. It is no exaggeration to suggest the railway created Windermere town which grew with amazing speed between the station and the lake, a booming of 19th century residential development. Perhaps Wordsworth had a point. What would Ambleside have looked like now if that had been the railway's terminus, and the wealthy merchants from Manchester and Liverpool had built their villas there?

The 10 mile branch leaves the fine canopied station of Oxenholme on the electrified West Coast main line (giving superb connections from almost every part of Britain). The little "Pacer" trains quickly swing along the hillside to Kendal, that most absorbing of northern towns, and then along the little green Kent valley to Burneside and Staveley. Both of them are old mill villages, the mills, particularily paper mills, taking advantage of the fast flowing River Kent for water power. You couldn't describe it as a spectacular journey - it's pleasant rather than breathtaking, with views of the hills with their craggy, spikey summits so characteristic of the Lakeland slatey rocks. Yet, hardly do you know it, before you're in the very heart of the Lake District National Park, within a short walk, from any of the little stations, of the most consumately beautiful landscape of England. But then that's what this particular railway is all about.

The Garburn Pass

THE WALK

Alight at Staveley. For most people travelling from beyond the branch, it's probably easiest to take a return ticket to Windermere, Staveley being only one station short of the terminus.

Go down the steps at the rear of the station platform by the Station Inn, turning left into the village and the busy main A591 Windermere road. Traffic apart, Staveley's an attractive mixture of the residential and early industrial, with a stream, complete with footbridge, through the village centre. On a more practical level, if you've been travelling some time, there are shops and a cafe to your right, public toilets to the left, and even a useful little grocery shop straight ahead.

Cross the road and head along the lane signed to Kentmere, past the above mentioned grocery shop, and soon passing Kentmere Mill, a still flourishing paper and cardboard factory, with a large mill pond.

The Kentmere Valley

Keep along the lane, now following the narrow Kentmere Valley. At the road junction, follow the lane to the left, marked No Through Road and signed for Browfoot, $1^1/_4$ miles (2km). This is a narrow, attractive way by the riverside, soon passing, at Fellfoot, cottages of considerable charm with Lakeland gardens to match and, as you climb a little, delightful views of the Kentmere Valley.

At the crossroads above Browfoot, turn right to descend to the farm, keeping ahead on the stoney track between farm buildings, before bearing left below the barns, along a track now following the valley bottom. At the next junction by a fine old station bridge - Ulthwaite Bridge - turn left uphill, along a narrowing track to Croft Head house, 50 metres beyond which you should fork right on the track down to Saw Mill Cottage. The path now goes left below the garden, over a footbridge and along an enclosed way between metal fences. Bear right in front of a cottage onto a tarmac drive, following this as it swings away up the valley. Ahead is a factory belonging to BISMIN, British Industrial Sand. Keep straight ahead between tall concrete corrugated iron buildings in the factory yard. This leads to a track soon passing woodland and an attractive mill pond offering superb views along its length to the head of the valley and the crags above Kentmere. You'll probably see swans gliding across the reflecting waters.

Where the track bears right at a fork, keep to the narrower, grassy path left. This goes over a step stile to become a beautiful grass path above the lake - again superb views ahead to Kentmere, in its magnificent setting of fells.

The path broadens to a track and enters Hall Wood, a deciduous woodland. Keep the same direction as other tracks join through the wood, until the track bears right through a gate and descends to ford a stream with helpful stepping stones for the rambler.

Immediately to the left is Kentmere Hall, a magnificent example of a Lakeland Pele Tower or fortified house, dating from the 14th century at a time when the North of England was plagued by Scottish raids.

Go through the gate ahead, then through the gate immediately to the right, the way marked with a footpath sign. You cross to the small gate in the top right hand corner of the field, ahead. Bear right to the larger boulder and barn ahead, and through the gate onto a farm track.

The Garburn Pass

But almost immediately, turn left again along the steep track which is signposted as a public bridleway. This stony way is the ancient Garburn Pass between Kentmere and the Troutbeck valley, busy in days of packhorse traffic, but little changed in appearance over the centuries. It is an extremely steep climb, up a hill which still keeps its old name of Crabtree Brow, but your exertions will quickly be rewarded by ever more splendid views of the crags and fell summits as you ascend.

Take your time. In every sense, the Garburn Pass forms the high point of this walk, and the murderously steep gradient only levels out for a short section before the final summit ascent.

But a real pass summit it is, marked by a field wall and gate, and once on top the most thrilling Lakeland panorama with, if it is clear, the Scafell range, Great Gable, the Langdales, and other peaks stretched out around you.

Nor does the sense of drama decline as you descend the track which swings into the Troutbeck valley - Kirkstone Pass, and its little line of toy-sized vehicles comes into view, and with it Helvellyn, and, as you turn the corner, a superb view of Windermere.

Continue along the track - here known as the Garburn Road - down the hillside, soon passing a disused quarry. At a junction in the tracks, take the higher route, to the left, Dubbs Road, which winds its way into a little valley, soon passing Dubbs Reservoir, and offers some fine, if less spectacular views to the left before reaching a junction into a lane.

Orrest Head

Turn right here for some 250 metres before reaching a steep step stile by a footpath sign on the left. Cross, following the field wall round to a ladder stile before bearing half left to a gap, then cross to another ladder stile you'll find in the far left corner of the next field. Go sharp right over this stile along along the wall to Near Orrest farm. The right of way goes through three little gates to a little cottage green within the farm complex. Turn left to the gate bearing right into the lane.

Keep right on the lane for 150 metres to a gate, left, which leads to a stile by a second gate with a footpath sign and path over a little footbridge. You are now on a grassy path which climbs uphill towards the summit of Orrest Head. Go through the stile to the summit, a magnificent little viewpoint which makes a fitting climax to this walk, merely a taste of what the Lake District has to offer, but filled with a sense of high drama nonetheless as you look down on Windermere and that breathtaking panorama of hills. There's also a couple of benches on which to collect your breath and a viewfinder to help name the great ring of hills.

The descent is easy enough. Follow the main path down, zigzagging from the summit crag (keep to the main path to help reduce erosion) before it bears left, losing itself in dense shrubbery and woodland above Elleray Bank before joining the metalled track which eventually emerges at the cross roads below Windermere station. A good choice of pubs, cafes, and shops is not too far away (including a Supermarket in the old station) before your diesel rail car whisks you away from the imaginatively refurbished little station back along the 10 miles of single track to Oxenholme and your InterCity express.

Unless, of course, you have been tempted to stay a little longer in this ramblers' paradise.

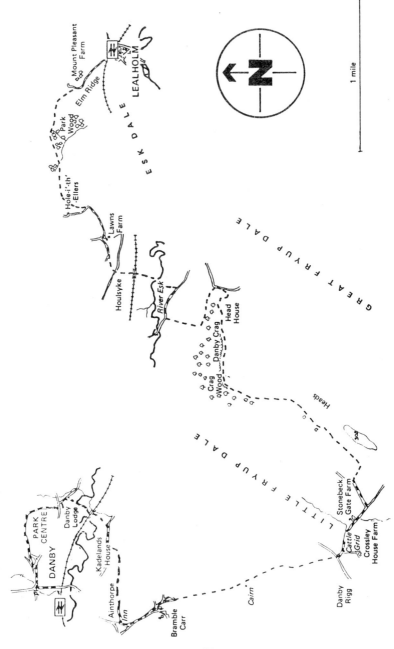

1 mile

WALK ELEVEN: The Esk Valley

Landranger Map: Sheet 94

Outdoor Leisure Map: Sheet 26 North York Moors (East)

Starting Station: Danby

Finishing Station: Lealholm

Distance: 9 miles (14.5 km)

Time required: 4 hours

Grade: Easy.

Possible Cut-Off Point: No suitable point.

Terrain: Fieldpaths, moorland paths, farm tracks.

Refreshment and accommodation facilities: pubs in Danby, Ainthorpe and Lealholm. Cafe at Danby Lodge National Park Centre and cafes at Lealholm.

Tourist Information: The Moors Centre, Danby (0287) 60654 *or* New Quay Road, Whitby (0947) 602674

THE RAIL JOURNEY

The 35 mile long Esk Valley railway is one of the few truly rural branch lines left in Britain, a meandering single-track route connecting isolated villages in the North York Moors National Park between Middlesbrough and Whitby, the solitary survivor of a whole network of branch lines in the area. The curious reversal at Battersby Junction is a relic of when this section of line was part of a through route from Picton on the main Northallerton-Middlesbrough line, with a link, at Battersby and its former Incline, with the celebrated Rosedale Ironstone Railway, now part of history and the 40 mile Lyke Wake Walk that uses part of the old trackbed over the Moors.

Lealholm Station, Eskdale

The Esk Valley line's survival owes much to the steepness of the terrain around villages like Egton and Glaisdale, where buses could not operate along the steep and narrow lanes, particularily during the winter months, and it still provides an important and socially necessary link, carrying people to and from work, schoolchildren and shoppers into Whitby or Middlesbrough. But it also provides a lifeline for the old port and holiday resort of Whitby, and, as one of Britain's most scenic lines, a superb way of enjoying the scenery of the North York Moors National Park, the large number of surviving village stations offering a huge choice of walks.

This particular walk was chosen because not only does it provide an opportunity to visit the Moors Centre at Danby Lodge - an excellent introduction into this unique area - but it gives a real flavour of the wild moorland landscape which is the essence of this National Park, where ancient civilisations never seem far away, and yet where sheltered, cultivated valleys contain a traditional English landscape.

THE WALK

Alight at the little halt of Danby which, in common with other stations on the Esk Valley line, has a "Welcoming" board on the platform with local information, jointly provided by British Rail and the National Park Authority to help orientate the visitor.

Turn left from the station into the little village centre, dominated by its extensive greens. There's a post office and the Duke of Wellington pub to delay you, but otherwise turn right at the crossroads beyond the higher green, continuing past a row of traditional cottages.

Where there's an area of open land, left, past these cottages, take the track left, and where this track forks, bear right, behind a stone house with its garden and greenhouses, soon crossing between gorse and bracken, climbing along the track. There are fine views from here into Eskdale. At a crossing of tracks, leave the track to follow a narrower path alongside the drystone wall, now descending to a gate, turning sharp right into a shallow little valley, and gate (waymarked) into a wood, a beautiful section of path. This goes through a gate at the road. Almost opposite is Danby Lodge.

The Moors Centre

Look for a little pedestrian gate on the right which leads into this fascinating country house turned National Park Centre, with its displays, exhibitions, information facilities and cafeteria, and attractive surrounding lawns.

There is plenty to see here, and you might well use up a full hour, so build in this time factor on your schedule.

Your route from the Centre is through the gate at the far side of the garden area, back onto the main road, but almost immediately past the centre through the waymarked path (one of the trails from the Centre) right, which follows the estate boundary, with fine views of the Lodge, to cross the River Esk at a metal footbridge. Keep ahead alongside pasture to the crossing over the railway line. Ahead to a stile into the lane.

Ainthorpe

Go right in the lane, and immediately past Kadelands House farm ahead, turn sharp left over a tiny bridge and stile along a signed path along the edge of a field, but at the top of the field ignore the sign "Castle Footpath" and turn right to a waymarked stile in the far corner. Continue alongside the wall, and through the gate at the end. Keep alongside the next wall, this time going through a gate into a narrow green lane. Follow this lane into Ainthorpe, another pleasant little village dominated like so many Moors villages, by an extensive village green. There's also the Fox and Hounds Inn to the left.

Continue past the pub, along the lane by tennis courts. Just before a bend in the lane, right, take the narrow, stony path, signed as a bridleway, which leaves the road and goes straight on, soon winding through gorse to a gate, then entering open moor.

Bronze Age Circle

You now follow a superb track over heather, gloriously purple in late summer, which ascends the side of Danby Rigg (Rigg being the dialect word, from old Norse, for moorland ridge), with impressive views from all sides as you climb.

You soon reach the remains of a small prehistoric circle or barrow, with a single, surviving five foot high standing stone. This circle was once some 42 feet (6^1/$_2$ metres) in diameter, and two important urn burials were excavated from the site, dating from 1, 000 BC. The barrow is one of many such on ridge tops on the Moors, often by the side of an old path or track, such as this one, like ancient waymarks, perhaps the burial ground of some forgotten prince.

The path now curves over the summit of Danby Rigg, and you look across into the heartland of the National Park, a vast, lonely landscape, primitive, forbidding, but immeasurably grand. Ahead is the beautiful, green valley of Little Fryup Dale.

The Two Fryups

The name "Fryup" has nothing to do with frying eggs or bacon, but derives from the Old English woman's name Friga, together with "hop" a small valley. These two little valleys, side valleys of Esk Dale, are amongst the loveliest on the Moors.

Descend the gently sloping green track into Little Fryup Dale to a cross roads. Walk along the lane, crossing the little stream that forms the dale, soon passing Stonebeck Gate Farm on the left. About 200 metres beyond the farm, go through a gate left onto a green lane, where harebells flourish in summer. About 200 metres along this lane, the bridleway goes through another gate, right, up another green lane which climbs to a little pine wood above. Follow the path left here, by tussocky grass and bracken, soon becoming a stony track which climbs and follows the mooredge.

There are particularily good views from here, across Little Fryup Dale, and beyond into the main Esk Valley.

The path now follows the top of a fine wood, with some birch and rowan trees. Follow the path round, above Danby Crags before eventually it swings across, as a track, to Head House Farm. Go through the gate, slightly left through the farmyard, swinging down the farmtrack with fine views now into Great Fryup Dale (the great being merely comparative) another lovely green little valley.

Before you reach the lane, however, bear left, through the broom and bracken, the wall below you, picking up the line of a green track. Follow it round, this time going below the wood, taking care to keep straight ahead, alongside the wall. The way now turns sharp right to a gate, going alongside fields - fine views of Houlsyke ahead. At the end of the field cross to the gate in the lane at an old layby, turning right in the lane for 200 metres, before going left, at a footpath sign, along a grassy track to the river where you cross at a wooden bridge. Go straight across the middle of the field to a metal gate at the pedestrian crossing over the railway. Cross with care, continuing straight ahead to a stile at the road.

Hole i' th' Ellers

The next path begins almost directly opposite. In this section of the walk the pathfinding needs care, but recent improvements to the foopath by the National Park and by voluntary teams have made things very much easier. Bear right in the field to the higher of two stiles in the wall, which leads, above another field wall, to a gate at Lawns Farm. The right of way now slopes left up a narrow enclosed way above the farm, before zigzagging back down a second enclosed way which emerges past the farm. Keep ahead now along the line of the path marked by field gates, across fields to a tiny ruined barn. You are now heading for the little farmhouse, romantically named Hole i' th' Ellers above left, and whilst there is a stile in the field wall above, in a straight line to the farm, it might be easier to avoid a growing crop to follow the fieldtrack, left, which goes round the outside and then along the top of the field to the farm. Go through this deserted farm, keep ahead alongside the fieldwall to a fieldgate on the right.

Go through here, heading for a gate down the pasture which leads across a little bridge over the stream in to the wood. Keep the same direction, almost due east, following the top of the next wood, Park Wood, at the end of which there is a stile and gate. Turn right through here, away from the wood and, downhill, but curving away below the line of the hedge above a shallow valley. Keep the little stream that forms the valley about 50 metres to your left. Eventually you go through a gate on the right to the other side of the hedge and a gate ahead to join a track from Greystones Farm, which itself joins a broad green way down Elm Ridge.

Lealholm

Almost before you are aware of it you are going through an old North Eastern Railway gate and you are at Lealholm Station, so perfectly situated at the end of the footpath.

Unless time for your return train is very short, give yourself the opportunity to explore this particularily delightful Moors village, easily reached by footpath direct from the station. There are cafes, a pub, craft shops, a garden nursery, loos, an 18th century bridge, stepping stones, another splendid village green and, on the little Methodist Chapel, carvings by John Castillo, an early Methodist preacher, one of the band of followers known as the "Lantern Saints" because they preached by the light of horn lanterns.

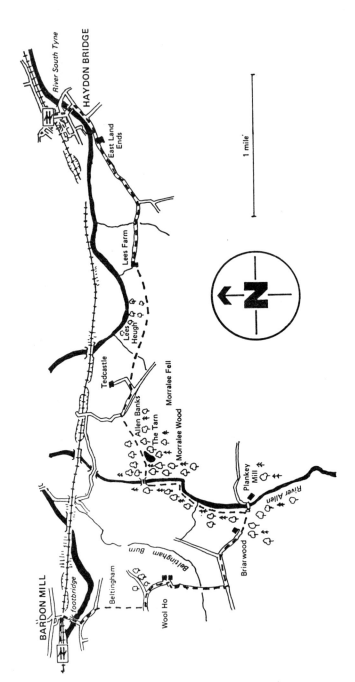

WALK TWELVE: Allen Banks

Landranger Map: Sheet 87

Pathfinder Map: Sheets NY 66/76, NY 86/96

Starting Station: Haydon Bridge

Finishing Station: Bardon Mill

Distance: 8 miles (12km)

Time required: 4 hours

Grade: moderate.

Possible Cut-Off Point: No suitable point.

Terrain: Lane, tracks, woodland and fieldpaths. Two steep uphill stretches, but otherwise fairly easy going.

Refreshment and accomodation facilities: Haydon Bridge pubs, shops, cafes. Facilities more limited at Bardon Mill to single public house (Bowes Arms)

Tourist Information: Sycamore Street, Haltwhistle (0498) 20351 *or* Hallgate, Hexham (0434) 605225

THE RAIL JOURNEY

The Tyne Valley Line between Carlisle and Newcastle, connecting as it does two important town and rail junctions on the West and East coast main lines respectively, and the only east-west cross country route between Tyneside and Cumbria, has great strategic importance. It is, nevertheless, something of an important rural lifeline, serving as it does the town of Hexham and a large hinterland of magnificent Border country, more or less parallel to the Roman Wall, and close to the boundaries of the Northumberland National Park.

Scenically, it is superb. From the suburbs of Newcastle to the fringes of Carlisle, the rail traveller enjoys fine views from both sides of the carriage window, to the east dominated by the rich beauty of Tynedale itself, to the west the watershed between the Tyne and Cumbria's River Eden looking across, from the train, into the hills of Scotland.

South Tyne Valley, near Haydon Bridge

Because the line's 62 miles link east and west so conveniently, it's possible to do this walk from either direction, catching one of the comfortable little "Pacer" diesels which provide the frequent service. But not all trains serve Bardon Mill in particular, so you'll need to make sure you've checked your return times.

THE WALK

A Town around a Bridge

Haydon Bridge has long been an important crossing point across the south Tyne. The lovely old multi-arched bridge over the Tyne, around which the town has developed, is now closed to vehicular traffic, the main A69 now crossing by a new concrete structure, leaving the ancient narrow bridge for pedestrians. But the town undoubtedly has Anglo-Saxon origins, the remains of the great Northumbrian Saint Cuthbert having been deposited for a time in the 9th century at Haydon Old Church, an Anglo-Saxon Church sited not far from the town. Stone from this building was used in the present, late 18th century church, also dedicated to Saint Cuthbert. There are two medieval gravestone covers from the old church in the present building.

The little town has shops, a couple of pubs; as facilities in Bardon Mill are minimal, it's a good idea to get any essential supplies here.

From the station proceed along the town down Church street, at the end of which an underpass goes under the busy A69 onto the old bridge to the southern part of the town. Turn right into Shaftoe street, walking along the street for 200 metres until, where the road sweeps away to the left, you must bear right along the narrower lane signed to Land End and Deanwood.

Tynedale Views

As the lane rises, and you leave the town and a caravan site behind, you enjoy the first of many views across the south Tyne Valley and surrounding hills, a mixture of pasture, scattered woodland and high moorland, typical Northumbrian countryside, not unlike the Yorkshire Dales to the south, but a broader, wilder kind of landscape.

As the road turns left, keep ahead along the farm track, a wooden sign indicating Lees and Allendale. You pass the farm and into a broad, cobblestone and grass area. Turn left, in front of cottages to the field gate, going sharp right alongside a wire fence, climbing steadily uphill to a gate ahead. The right of way is about 50 metres to the left of the fence, but a gate ahead is a more obvious and easy place to cross the wall than the difficult to find stile. Keep in the same direction, behind an attractive birch wood, to a gate in the wall not far from the wood corner. Go through here, the path following the inside of another wall, now with more superb views up the Tyne on the far side of the low headland.

The path follows the wall, cutting across from the point where the wall bends left, to cross the wall ahead, but again, the gate in the bottom of the field is an easier crossing point. Keep ahead on the track to a gate leading into the drive from Tedcastle Farm. Turn left here, uphill to the lane. Go right in the lane below the wood to a gateway and National Trust sign on the left.

Allen Banks - a woodland paradise

Go through the little pedestrian gate, heading to the left of the clump of pines ahead to locate a faint green track which enters, by another pedestrian gate and fire warning notice, a deep and rich woodland, with a mixture of pine, birch, oak and rhododendron through which the paths run.

Allen Banks Estate consists of 194 acres of woodland and crag scenery given to the National Trust by Frances Bowes Lyon, a relative of the Queen Mother, to the Trust in 1942, with additional parts of the Ridley Estate added to the property in later years.

The path climbs to a beautiful hidden Tarn, deep in Morralee Wood, its waterside benches a temptation for meditation. Immediately beyond the Tarn are more dramatic views into Tynedale, this time encompassing Ridley Hall, former seat of the Ridleys, a Tynedale family whose most famous member was Bishop Nicholas Ridley, 1500-55, burnt at the stake for his Protestant beliefs in the time of Queen Mary I.

Beyond the Tarn the ways fork. Take the left fork which ascends through more rhododendrons, turning right at the top, then bearing right at a junction to another woodland path. Go left here down steps to another fine viewpoint before turning right along the path which zigzags down through the woods, keeping left at the next junction to where steps, right, lead to a narrow wire cable bridge over the River Allen. Don't worry too much if you miss any of these paths. If you follow the white marker posts you will soon meet on the main path through the woods, this follows a trail in a large loop which, in any direction, descends to the swing bridge. Just give yourself plenty of time to enjoy this beautiful, richly wooded gorge, dominated by mature beech and Scots pine trees, together with birch, elm, ash, alders and even junipers.

Cross the little swing bridge with care, turn left along the broad track which follows the riverside, up river, at one point climbing away from the river edge, then, skirting the well named Raven Crag, a mixture of limestone and soft sandstone, and lovely pine woodland, you are back to the river edge. After half a mile or so, you reach a footbridge across a narrow gill, leading to a rocky headland. Follow the path as it winds left over this headland and descends to another long narrow swing bridge, this time leading to Plankey Mill.

Plankey Mill

Though all signs of the mill and its mill race have long vanished, this remains an attractive picnic and parking area close to the river, with enticing paths leading further up the riverside.

But for Bardon Mill retrace your steps back over the swing bridge to the footbridge, going sharp left immediately over this bridge into the Northumberland Naturalists Trust's Briarwood Banks Nature Reserve. The path climbs very steeply up by a narrow ravine. Keep right where the ways fork, climbing out of the valley, right again at the junction of paths, to emerge at a kissing gate above the wood, below Briarwood Farm. Keep ahead, to the left of farm buildings where you'll see a stile by the farm gate leading to the farm drive. Follow this track as it winds round to join the lane.

Wool House

Turn left in the lane, which is an ancient road known as Ward Way, probably used by leadminers in previous centuries. You soon pass a plantation on the left, at the opposite end of which there is a gate on the right. Ignore this, continuing for another 100 metres or so to the next gate on the right. Go through here, the path now following the wall along a faint track, the wall to your left, again with lovely views across Tynedale with, in the distance, if it is clear, Hadrian's Wall itself clearly visible on the high moorland ridge above Crag Lough - by Housesteads Fort.

Where you come to three gates, take the middle one, ahead, the wall now on your right, along a faint, green way. This descends to Wool House Farm. Go right through the gate into the farmyard then through the next gate, left, into the farm drive. The name of this farm, situated on the edge of the now enclosed Ridley Common, indicated its age-old connection with sheep farming.

Bardon Mill

Follow this attractive winding way to a junction of tracks east of Shaws Farm. Go sharp left here towards the farm, but about 20 metres before the farmhouse look for a gap stile in the wire fence, right, between two narrow fence posts. This marks the line of the right of way across the pasture. This descends to the bottom of the field - keep the narrow wood and burn to the left, skirting boggy areas at the bottom of the field around some old mysterious earthworks with half hidden walls. At the bottom corner of the field is a hurdle stile. Cross, fording the tiny stream. and keeping to the edge of the field below the wood to locate a stone step stile in the wall corner. This leads to the lane corner. Keep ahead for a 100 metres or so to reach the long narrow footbridge over the Tyne which emerges at the very edge of Bardon Mill Station.

The original Bardon Mill on the side of Brackies Burn which descends from the edge of the Roman Wall to the Tyne, has long vanished, but of interest in the town is a pottery specialising in the firing of traditional chimney pots and glazed garden pots. Apart from the post office and pub there are few facilities so time your walk well to avoid too long a wait at the little station.

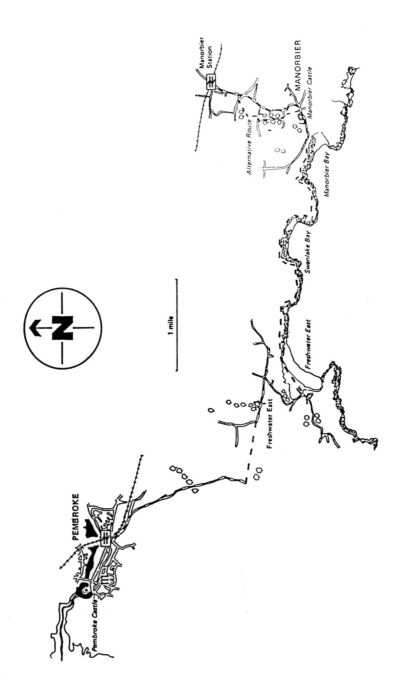

WALK THIRTEEN: Pembrokeshire Coast

Landranger Map: Sheet 158

Pathfinder Map: Sheet SS 09/19

Starting Station: Pembroke

Finishing Station: Manorbier

Distance: $10^1/_2$ miles (17 km)

Time Required: Allow at least five hours.

Grade: Moderate.

Possible Cut-Off Point: Freshwater East 3 miles (5 km) with a walk along lanes to Lamphey station.

Terrain: Fieldpaths through lush pastures, but coastal paths section has numerous steep climbs and descents requiring care.

Refreshment and Accommodation: Cafes, shops, pubs, guest house and hotel accommodation in Pembroke and nearby Tenby. Limited amount of accommodation on route at Freshwater East and Manorbier. Several camp sites nearby. A Youth Hostel approximately $1/_2$ mile from Saundersfoot railway station.

Tourist Information: Guildhall, Tenby (0834) 2402/3510

THE RAIL JOURNEY

The journey from Cardiff, capital of Wales, to Pembroke, provides delightful variety. The train sweeps by industrial towns like Port Talbot and Neath, before reaching Swansea, Wales' second largest city. Once a major port, its spacious new city centre is largely a result of rebuilding after horrifying damage in the Second World War. But it is only really when you reach Ferryside that you begin to enjoy fine views. The Afon Tywi comes in to sight with Llanstephan Castle guarding the swirling tidal waters. This is Dylan Thomas country and a few miles up the road is Laugharne, where the Swansea-born poet (1914-53) lived for a number of years. The train pauses at Carmarthen, an important market town, famous for its castle and as the legendary birthplace of Merlin, King Arthur's wizard, before travelling through rich dairy farming country to Whitland where the branch for Pembroke Dock begins.

The Pembrokeshire Coast

It's a little over 27 miles from the junction at Whitland to Pembroke Dock. Built as a single line, initially to Tenby before being extended to

Pembroke Dock, it was completed by 1864, having had a struggle to obtain authorisation through Parliament owing to rival schemes. The hope was that the line would serve a number of purposes, in particular feed traffic to the docks, but also stimulate the growth of Tenby as a holiday resort. Excursion trains brought important traffic on the line and even today there are InterCity trains on summer Saturdays for holidaymakers.

From Whitland, the train makes its way through Lampeter Vale to Narberth, a small settlement huddled around the Norman castle, then on to Kilgetty and Saundersfoot. Now a fashionable yachting harbour, it was once busy exporting Welsh anthracite to France, Spain and Germany. The Saundersfoot Railway and Harbour Company even built a narrow guage tramway to get coal down to the boats from Kilgetty. This region of West Wales, formerly Pembrokeshire but now incorporated into the County of Dyfed, was sometimes referred to as "Little England beyond Wales" because its people were English rather than Welsh speaking.

Tenby, with its medieval town walls and streets, beautiful beaches and prominent castle overlooking the harbour, is attractive at any time of the year. There is a museum built into the castle walls and the Tudor Merchant's House is also open to the public. Between Tenby and Penally, there are views of the sea and Caldey Island which is inhabited by Cistercian monks who make perfume and pottery. Boat trips are run from Tenby in the summer, but only men are allowed the full guided tour of the monastery! They are currently reported to be on the look-out for suitable recruits to join their tiny band.

From Penally, the train follows an inland route through to Manorbier and Lamphey. Near to Lamphey Station is the ruined Lamphey Palace open to the public, and Lamphey Court, a splendid Georgian mansion, now a hotel.

The heart of Pembroke town is Main Street, one long medieval way leading to the castle. Pembroke Castle is one of the most impressive Norman castles in Britain. Seated on a craggy rock and overlooking the Pembroke River, this fortification has resisted many an uprising. The Keep is massive; it is said to have walls 19 feet thick at its base. On the northern side, there is secret access to the Inner Ward by way of a natural cave "The Wogan" from the river. You'll also be able to view the remains of the ancient town walls and three medieval churches, as well as the traditional shops and town houses. It is worth spending some time to stroll around the town before the walk. Pembroke has an atmosphere which is particularly appealing.

THE WALK

Bear left off the station platform, left again under the bridge to the traffic roundabout. If you plan to visit Pembroke town (allow at least an hour) go straight on at the roundabout into the town centre, returning to this same roundabout to rejoin the walk.

To Freshwater East

From the roundabout, go left (coming from the station) into Lower Lamphey Road. After half a mile, you turn right opposite some imposing houses with a post box on the left. This tarmac lane leads to Lammaston Farm. Go to the right of the farm buildings, then curve left, then right, in front of the farmhouse. This lane becomes a muddy track and will shortly lead to a sharp left hand turn. Go through the barred gate and continue with the banked hedge to your left, crossing three enclosures then proceeding mid field to a barred gate at Porthclew Corner. Walk the short distance along this road to Freshwater East. At the cross roads, bear right and follow the road down to cafe, shop and toilets. Your way is waymarked to the left through the dunes. Alternatively, you can walk along the seashore instead. Either way, it is easy to pick up the coastal path at the eastern end of the beach.

Freshwater East itself is perhaps a little ordinary, but the beach and coastal views are magnificent. This is a convenient cut-off point if you decide not to continue to Manorbier. Retrace your steps to the crossroads, but instead of turning left onto the B4584, go straight across onto the quiet minor road passing Halls Lake Farm. Ignore the right turn at the first junction. At the second, bear left and right at the crossroads in Lamphey.

Coastal Path

The ramble follows the clearly defined Pembrokeshire Coastal Path, one of Britain's Long Distance Footpaths for about $2^1/_2$ miles(4 km), well and truly in the Pembrokeshire Coast National Park. It is a steep climb up to West Moor Cliff and an equally severe descent to the secluded Swanlake Bay. Rugged cliffs and broad bays and windswept hedgerows characterise this area. Continue on to East Moor Cliff, an even steeper climb, then finally to Manorbier Bay. Pass by a house named The Dak and your way is upwards to the tarmac road.

Geraldus Cambrensis

The castle, soon reached on your left, is a private residence, but is open to the public in summer. It was the home of a celebrated medieval scholar, Geraldus Cambrensis (which roughly translated means "Gerald the Welshman") who became a 12th century Rector of Tenby and Archdeacon of Brecon, one of the greatest Welsh historians and travel writers of his day.

There are a couple of inns in the village, a post office and shop. The walk to the station is along roads which are fairly quiet except at the height of the season. Allow half an hour or more for this. As you walk by the castle, bear left and follow this road (B4585) until you reach the main A4139. Cross over and bear left, then immediately right, by a white cottage to the lane leading to the station.

(As an alternative to using these roads from the village, busy in summer, you can take the waymarked field paths to Park Farm and on to Norton Farm, leaving only a short stretch of road walking from the junction of the A4139 to Manorbier Station. The route is clearly waymarked throughout, but requires a little more time.)

The arrival of a train at Manorbier is quite an event as the guard has to open and close the level crossing gates.

This is still a very rural railway !

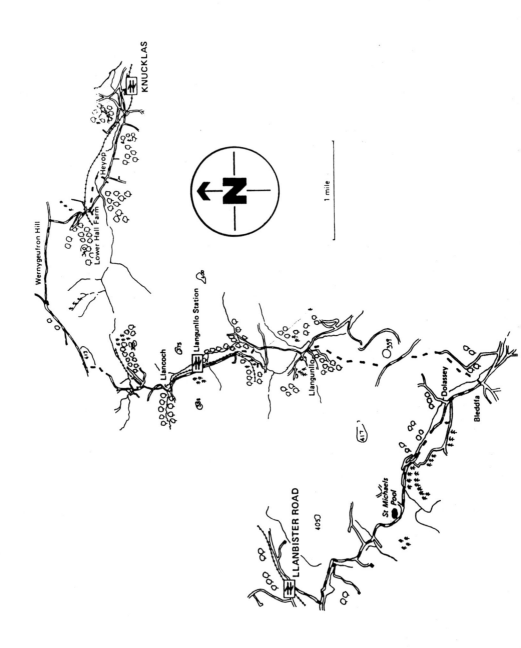

KNUCKLAS

Hevop

Wernygeufron Hill

Lower Hall Farm

417

Llancoch

Llangunllo Station

Llangunllo

359

417

Dolassey

Bleddfa

LLANBISTER ROAD

405

St Michaels Pool

1 mile

N

WALK FOURTEEN: The Heart of Wales

Landranger Map: Sheet 148

Pathfinder Map: Sheet SO27/37

Starting Station: Llanbister Road

Finishing Station: Knucklas

Distance: 11 miles (18 km)

Time Required: Allow at least $6^1/2$ hours.

Grade: Moderate to strenuous.

Possible Cut-Off Point: Llangynllo station $6^1/2$ miles(10km)

Terrain: Hilly sheep farming country, with many of the paths little used.

Refreshment and Accommodation: Two key locations on the route - Llandrindod Wells and Knighton, otherwise facilities restricted. There is a Youth Hostel at Knighton.

Tourist Information: The Old School, Knighton (0547) 528753/528529 *or* Rock Park Spa, Llandrindod Wells (0597) 2600

THE RAIL JOURNEY

One of the remotest and grandest railway routes in Britain, the Heart of Wales Line is held in great affection by many a railway traveller. Its 90 miles of single track from Craven Arms to Llanelli traverse some magnificent countryside. Highlights include views of the Brecon Beacons and Cambrian Mountains, of the infant Twyi and Wye rivers, of the hill farms and sheltered hamlets that roll by as the train picks its way between the hills. Whether you travel down from Shrewsbury, or up from Llanelli, you won't be disappointed by this spectacular rail journey.

Knucklas Viaduct

The great railway builders of the 19th century had high expectations from this line - it would not only be a major trunk route between the industrial North of England and the South Wales coalfields, but also a link to ocean-going vessels bound from Swansea to New York. The line was, in the event, built piecemeal by four separate companies who were eventually merged into the London and North Western Railway, but retaining a degree of partnership with the Great Western Railway at the southernmost end. The key towns on route are Knighton, Llandrindod Wells, Llandovery and Llandeilo, all busy market towns, still attracting shoppers by train from intermediate rural halts.

Llandrindod Wells

The railway also attracted those seeking treatment at the spas Llanwrtyd and Llangammarch Wells and Llandrindod. The latter proved to be the most popular. Even in the 1980s, Victorian and Edwardian elegance remain. The boating lake, ornamental gardens, Pavilion and restored Rock Park Spa Pump Room all add to the setting. The Pump Room houses an exhibition area, the Tourist Information centre and an Edwardian Tea Room. The manageress serves three tasty spa waters - magnesium, sulphur, and saline (salt) by handpump - all excellent for tired livers!

The highlight of Llandrindod's year is the annual Victorian Festival, when the clock turns back a full century and everyone in town dresses in like their great grandfather or grandmother. For details, contact the Tourist Information Centre.

On many trains on the Heart of Wales Line, more passengers will board at Llandrindod than from the rest of the unstaffed stations to Craven Arms added together. Rural depopulation, increased car ownership and a drop in patronage led eventually to proposals for closure which were resisted. But local community groups and a thriving line association has done much to assist British Rail in the marketing of the line, particularly for leisure traffic. Ask the train guard for a ticket to Llanbister Road. A few years ago he might have been surprised, but not nowadays !

THE WALK

A true optimist named this one Llanbister, for the village is a full 5 miles along that road away. The station is, in fact, more convenient for Llangynllo. You'll notice the silence that falls after the train has gone.

Turn left out of the station and then over the bridge before bearing right. At the farm complex bear left. This tarmac lane becomes a track climbing its way up to the top of the ridge. Ignore turns off to the left and right. Once over the brow of the hill, there is a house on the left and St Michael's Pool. Ignore another turning to the left. Continue down the clearly defined track by the wood and as it veers off to the right, go through the barred gate on the left, passing by the derelict building on the left and continuing ahead towards the large barn at Dolassey. The path passes by the right of the barn and farm, continuing down a tarmac lane to Bleddfa. There is a street light on your left. That is your way to Llangynllo. You might like to take the opportunity to enjoy a refreshment stop at The Hundred House pub by the village green.

Land of Five Barred Gates

Retrace your steps to the turning by the street lamp. The path is signposted. Your way is down to a stream, over the footbridge and up the hillside by gorse bushes. This track soon peters out. Keep directly ahead through two barred gates onto open grassland, with an old quarry scar on your left. Your path curves round gently to the left through two barred gates. In the distance you can see another barred gate diagonally right across the large field. Tre-boeth Farm should be over the fields to your left. Go through the gate and bear left, keeping the fence to your left. Go through another gate, then, as you approach a fenced off green track, bear right down the valley side to beyond the field corner where there is a barred gate and a stream to go through. The track now starts to become better defined again. It rises slightly, curves and then descends gradually to the Lugg flood plain below. As you approach the farm buildings, just beyond the silage, go through the gate on the right and then follow the hedge on the left to the tarmac road.

Llangynllo

The village offers a post office, shop and The Greyhound pub, as well as an interesting mixture of houses. Bear right at the crossroads, go straight across at the next junction and as the lane bends to the right, go through the barred gate ahead, down to a foot bridge. The path leads upwards, slightly left, to the field edge and then to the tarmac lane. Bear right and continue to Llangynllo Station, one of the highest points on the line. This is a useful point to stop if you decide you've had enough and want to shorten the walk.

If carrying on, follow the lane past Llancoch Farm. Underneath is Llangynllo Tunnel, said to be haunted by the spirit of an engine driver from Knighton. This section of route uses part of Glyndwr's Way, a long distance footpath route through Mid Wales. The lane shortly begins to curve to the right and opposite a barn there is a path through the barred gate to the farm. Go through the farmyard, cross the ford and follow the track upwards, ignoring the first turn to the right, but continuing upwards. At the fork bear right, the track rising up gradually at first. In the next enclosure, head uphill again to a gate mid-field, then bear slightly left to a barred gate leading onto open moorland.

There are marvellous views from here across to Heyop Church and Knucklas Castle, which are not far away now. Turn right and walk along this spongy moorland covered in bracken. Keep to the fence on your right and after a mile, follow it as it begins to curve to the right. In approximately three quarters of a mile (just over 1 km), you will have to make a right turning. There are few landmarks to guide you so be vigilant.

Into the Heyop Valley

As you approach Goytre Hill, look out for the lane coming up from the left, and a solitary tree. Bear right, through the barred gate onto the track descending to Lower Hall Farm in the Heyop Valley below. The track passes an old quarry, zigzags down under the railway tunnel to the farm. Take a left turning by the fuel tanks into the field and continue ahead through the barred gate, keeping the hedge to the right. Bear right towards the stream bank, but if you have difficulty in getting through the hedge at this point, there is a gateway just to the left. Bear right here over the footbridge to a stile to the left of Heyop churchyard leading through a builders to the tarmac lane. Go left and follow the lane in to Knucklas village, dominated by the ruins of its 13th century castle. The village has a store, pub and the station is on the right above the council houses. There's a good view of Knucklas viaduct, perhaps one of the most impressive architectural features on the Heart of Wales Line, with its 13 stone arches and mock embattlements. Built to last, hopefully, like the rest of this magnificent line.

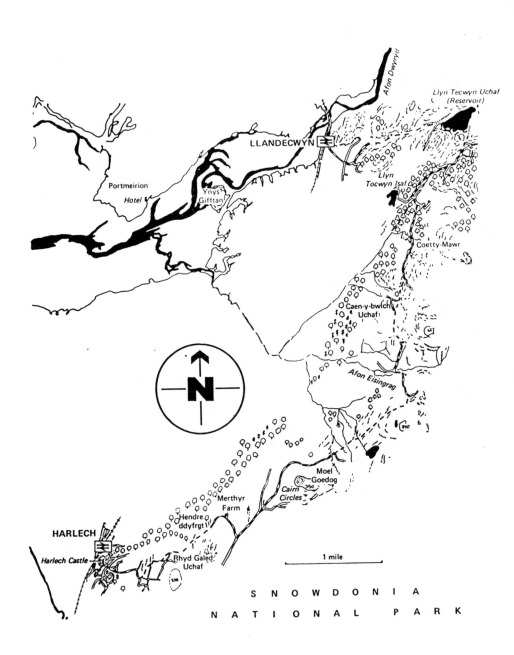

WALK FIFTEEN: Along the Cambrian Coast

Landranger Map: Sheet 124

Outdoor Leisure Map: Sheet 18 Snowdonia (Harlech and Bala)

Starting Station: Llandecwyn

Finishing Station: Harlech

Distance: 10 miles (16 km)

Time Required: Allow at least 6 hours.

Grade: Moderate to strenuous.

Possible Cut-Off Point: Llyn Tocwyn Isaf $2^1/_2$ miles (4 km), with a walk along lanes to Talsarnau.

Terrain: This is a walk through the westward hills of Meirionnydd, with some steep climbs and, in a few places, boggy conditions. Good footwear essential.

Refreshment and Accommodation: Cafes, shops, pubs, guest house and hotel accommodation in Harlech and also in the other towns up and down the line. Youth Hostel and camp site at Harlech.

Tourist Information: High Street, Harlech (0766)780658

THE RAIL JOURNEY

The Cambrian Coast line is justly renowned for its beauty, 53 miles of single track from Dovey Junction to the seaside resort of Pwllheli. Built in the 1860s, this magnificient line has resisted attempts to close it from the sea, several landslides and sundry bureaucracies, retaining the fiercely independent Welshness it had when it was part of The Cambrian Railway well over one hundred years ago.

A journey on the Cambrian Coast Line should really begin at Shrewsbury, a major junction in rural railway terms and a very pleasant place to change trains. The Cambrian Line, as the line that provides the first stage of our journey is usually known, is the main public transport artery into Mid Wales.

The first few miles from Shrewsbury cross lowland landscapes, but soon the line begins to climb to the Welsh Border, where spectacular scenery begins to unfold. First stop is Welshpool, the home of the 'Welshpool and Llanfair Light Railway', the Montgomeryshire Canal and Powis Castle. In the town, there's also a fine example of a brick cockpit once used for that most barbaric of sports. In between Newtown and Machynlleth, the countryside is exceptionally fine. The line's summit is reached at Talerddig, the track then descending to Cemmaes Road. Passengers very often change at Machynlleth, but the Cambrian Coast line really begins at the next station down the line, Dovey Junction.

Harlech Castle

It is sometimes necessary to change trains at the Junction - one of British Rail's most isolated halts; there is no road access - only estuary, marsh and wildfowl. The train eases its way over the bridge towards Aberdyfi passing the old bridgemaster's house, a reminder of a time when the bridge was opened for cargo vessels making their way further up the Dyfi to Derwentlas. This first section of the route from here to Aberdyfi is particularly scenic, and many would argue the best stretch of the line.

What makes this area so popular for holidays is without doubt its beauty, but also its history; harbours like Aberdyfi, Porthmadog and Barmouth; magnificient castles at Harlech and Criccieth; the narrow guage railways at Towyn, Fairbourne and Porthmadog. This more than makes up for the above average rainfall. On the other hand, the climate is mild and the vegetation lush. All the towns mentioned have stations close to their centres (except Porthmadog which is a good 10 minutes' walk). What is more intriguing is the way in which so many of the line's wayside halts have remained open. No doubt the transporting of children to local schools has played a big part, but also perhaps the growing interest in tourism and access to the countryside. Many of the wayside halts were opened late in the 1920s and 1930s. Llandecwyn is just such a halt, serving a mere handful of houses a quarter of a mile up the road. You reach it as the train speeds along a 4 mile straight stretch of track across the Morfa Harlech, a tenuous piece of land between sea and those devillish hills to your right, towards the estuary of the Afon Dwyryd, overlooked by Llandecwyn halt.

THE WALK

Alight at Llandecwyn, a short platform made of sleepers. Don't forget to give the guard advance notice, or the train is not likely to stop.

From the station bear right on the tarmac road, with the marshland on your right, and walk the short distance to the main A496 road. Cross over to the lane opposite and after approximately 150 metres, bear left by the second house on the left. Go through the white barred gate and proceed downwards along a well beaten track. This soon turns right, rising remorselessly up to Llyn Tecwyn Uchaf. There's a luxurious growth of bracken and the hillsides are covered with heather, a heavenly mauve in late summer. It all seems too good to be true, probably because

113

you've not yet seen the electricity transmission pylons plunging down this steep sided valley. Though an ugly intrusion, they are your guide posts; follow them up to the reservoir. Go through the barred gate to your right, then bear left, following the narrow and sometimes awkward path alongside the right hand bank of the reservoir to the ladder stile. Go over it, bear right and within a few metres, go through an iron gate. The path bears right again, and drops to a tarmac road by Tynffrwd cottage.

Ancient Oaks

Bear right onto the tarmac lane and follow it down the valley, clothed in ancient oaks, the sort of woodland that conservationists have been concerned to protect and with every justification. This is a magnificent landscape, and it seems almost inconceivable that such an upland habitat can play so great a host to many species of plants. In just under a mile, after a clearing on your left there is also a junction left, over the Afon y Glyn. If you are planning to complete the full walk, this is your route.

If you wish to shorten the walk, follow the tarmac lane beyond this junction, passing by Llyn Tocwyn Isaf and the hamlet of Bryn Bwbach. Continue ahead here, but bear right at the next junction. This lane leads you to Talsarnau village and Railway Halt.

Otherwise, having gone left, once over the cattle grid go right at the next junction following this up to an isolated farm, Coetty-Mawr. Just beyond the farmhouse bear right, instead of continuing ahead by the barn, then turn immediately left prior to the barred gate. Follow this track up to the brow, where it curves first to the right then left. Go through the gap, towards a derelict barn ahead of you in the adjacent field, then bear right passing by two small enclosures seen on your left. There are marvellous views to your right across the valley to Llandecwyn Plas Chapel and in the distance, the extraordinary Italianate village of Portmeirion, designed by Sir Clough Williams-Ellis, on the Dwyryd Estuary.

However, your immediate objective is to head across wet ground towards the homestead "Caen-y-blwch Uchaf". Walk towards the meeting point of two fiercesome looking drystone walls. There is, believe it or not, a stone stile at this point. Once over, the going is easier. Follow the path upwards beyond Caen-y-blwch Uchaf, to a natural gap through the hillside.

Prehistoric Circle

A new viewpoint opens out and the town of Harlech comes into sight for the first time. The path bears left here. Continue towards the house, then onto the track which soon meets a tarmac lane. At this point, you must bear left onto the access road up to Llyn Eiddew-mawr and Llyn Eiddew-bach. However, once beyond the first drystone wall, there is a path off to the right. It leads up to a barred gate. Go through it and bear right onto a well worn, ancient track across the moorland slopes for two to three miles towards Harlech. A very short climb first, then a gradual descent before rising once more to round Moel Goedog. On your right, you'll see a number of standing stones and a hut circle, evidence of early settlement in these foothills from over 2500 years ago.

Continue until the track meets the tarmac lane. Bear left and shortly the entrance of Merthyr Farm comes up on your right. Follow this through the caravan and camping area to the farm, where your way is marked by yellow arrows to the left of the farm buildings. Keep the drystone wall to your left and pass firstly a five barred gate then a smaller gate, passing by Hendre-ddyfrgi on the left to another small gate. Continue ahead through a series of small gates to a kissing gate and to a stile decorated by an iron bedstead. Follow the steps down by the spring to the first house, where you bear left at the gap in the fence. Now continue ahead to the right hand side of the cottages and on to a stone stile. Proceed, following the yellow waymarks, until a gap in the wall appears on the right above a barn. Walk down this walled lane, beyond the two cottages, and then along a clear path descending to the tarmac lane below. Bear right for the final section of the walk to the centre of Harlech.

Harlech

Harlech Castle, built on a high, wild crag, emanates sheer strength. It is reputed to be one of the best preserved castles in Wales, alongside Caernarfon and Conwy, and was built in the latter part of the 13th century by King Edward I. They are of international importance for their architectural splendours. But Harlech's history is as fascinating as its architecture. In the 15th century, it was the main base of the great Welsh nationalist leader Owain Glyndwr when he rose against the English, and in the English Civil War, it held out against Parliamentary forces until the end. Give yourself plenty of time for a visit - the Castle is open most days of the year.

Close by the Castle, you'll find numerous shops and cafes and below the embattlements on the seaward side of the railway station. Not too long before the railway was built, the sea lapped the lower edges of the castle. Now you'll have to walk another mile if you want to dip tired feet in the soothing brine.

LLANRWST

Gwydir Castle

Pont Fawr

Afon Conwy

Llyn Parc

Oakland:

Afon Leugwy

GWYDYR FOREST

BETWS-Y-COED

1 mile

Mon

Llyn Elsi Reservoir

Carnedd Moel-Siabod
- 2861 -

Afon Lledr

Craig Lledr

Gethin's Bridge

Lledr House

Dolwyddelan Castle (remains of)

Dolwyddelan

ROMAN BRIDGE

Bertheos

WALK SIXTEEN: Conwy and Lledr Valleys

Landranger Map: Sheet 115

Outdoor Leisure Map: Sheet 16 (Snowdonia - Conwy Valley)

Starting Station: Roman Bridge

Finishing Station: Llanrwst

Distance: 13 miles (21.5km)

Time Required: Allow 7 hours

Grade: Strenuous.

Possible Cut-Off Point: Dolwyddelan 2 miles(3km) *(Easy)*, or Betws-y-Coed 8 miles(13km) *(Moderate)*.

Terrain: Mainly field or moorland paths, with steep climbs in several places and indistinct paths on occasion.

Refreshments and Accommodation: Good supply of facilities in Betws-y-Coed and Llanrwst, plus accommodation on route. Youth Hostels at Pont-y-Pant in the Lledr Valley and also between Betws-y-Coed and Llanrwst.

Tourist Information: Castle Street, Conwy (049 263) 2248 *or* Royal Oak Stables, Betws-y-Coed (069 02) 426/665 *or* High Street, Blaenau Ffestiniog (0766) 830360

THE RAIL JOURNEY

For decades, people from Merseyside, Manchester and The Midlands have been taking the train to North Wales. All routes converge on Chester, a justifiably famous walled city, which makes it an ideal touring base for the rail traveller for North Wales and the Welsh Borders. The main line between Chester and Holyhead keeps for the most part close to the coastline, at first by the Dee Estuary, then the Irish Sea, so it is not uncommon for rail travellers on the coastal line to see boats making their way to Liverpool and in one or two places smaller vessels calling at isolated jetties mainly to take cargoes of stone aggregates.

Much of this coastal strip has been urbanised, with row upon row of seaside caravans and chalets destroying all sense of natural beauty. The traditional resorts of Prestatyn, Rhyl, Abergele and Colwyn Bay, all vying for holiday trade, eagerly await new arrivals from each train. But beyond the crowded coastline are superb hills, first the Clwyd range and then the mighty peaks and ranges of Snowdonia itself. Past Colwyn Bay, the countryside begins to open out around the railway line, and you change at Llandudno Junction from the main Chester-Holyhead line for the Blaenau Ffestiniog service into the heart of the Snowdonia National Park.

The Conwy Valley Line didn't start life as a recreational route. It was built in the 1860s to link the slate town of Blaenau Ffestiniog to the coast. Previously, most of the traffic was transported up or down the River Conwy and then by packhorse or waggon. But like so many of the other branch railways first opened up in mountainous areas for commercial traffic, the Conwy Valley Line also allowed growing numbers of ramblers and sightseeing tourists to reach magnificent countryside. Betws-y-Coed is a prime example of a tourist centre which owed everything to the railway. But even in the days of car competition, this branch line is by far the best way to enjoy the Conwy and Lledr valleys, with the roads in the summer season being very congested, particularly on Summer Sundays. It is for this reason that Gwynedd County Council operate the "Sunday Shuttle" charter rail service to supplement the Monday to Saturday BR service, giving a congestion-free way to enjoy the National Park, with superb views from the train. The reopening of the Ffestiniog railway line from Porthmadog into Blaenau, where a new station links both Conwy Valley line and the narrow gauge steam railway, has given the railway a new lease of life as part of one of the most exciting railway trips in Britain, from Llandudno right through to the Barmouth estuary.

Roman Pearls

Even from the platforms of Llandudno Junction, the impressive battlements of Conwy Castle can be seen across the waters. It is a splendid example of a medieval fortification and worth a visit if time permits - there is now a newly reopened station on the main line in Conwy, right under the ancient castle walls, or it's only a short walk from Llandudno Junction Station across the estuary bridge to the town.

Once on the branch, the train soon follows the estuary to Glan Conwy, once a thriving quayside, then on to Tal-y-Cafn a former ferry crossing. Across the river, you might notice an old church at Caerhun. It is just possible to make out earthworks here, thought to be the remains of a Roman fortress *Canovivm*. One reason suggested for its existence, is that the Romans were anxious to control the pearl business in the area, as pearls grew in the fresh water 'horse mussels' along this stretch.

The Red Giant

At this point, you become aware of the growing size of the surrounding mountains. On the left there is a rocky outcrop shaped like a chair. This is known as *Cadair Ifan Goch* for legend has it that a giant of this name would stand with one foot on this chair and the other on the opposite range and would wash his hands and face in the Conwy River.

Llanrwst Bridge

Ffestiniog Link

The train connects Llanrwst and Betws-y-Coed before climbing its way up the spectacular Lledr Valley. The final stretch is a very long tunnel emerging at Blaenau Ffestiniog, a town surrounded by mountains of slate. The slate mining centres of Llechwedd and Gloddfa Ganol are excellent places to explore. You can go down the specially reopened slate mines on foot, by underground tramway, or by the steepest underground railway in Britain.

Many people using this railway, take advantage of the Ffestiniog Circular Tour Ticket travelling on to Minffordd for a return journey along the Cambrian Coast. A trip on the Ffestiniog narrow gauge railway is a remarkable experience, specially designed steam locomotives hauling the little trains over mountainous territory to the coast, including the descent of the famous Dduallt loop, an Andes-style railway spiral, unique in the British Isles. If you can possibly afford the time, it's worth spending an extra day in this area to make the trip.

THE WALK

Alight at Roman Bridge, the easiest station name to pronounce on the line. It is thought that the bridge crossing the Lledr nearby was an early Roman route, hence the name. It is a request stop, so be sure to inform the guard that you wish to alight. From the station entrance, turn left along the tarmac road to the main A470. Bear left and walk along the main road for a short distance with great care as it can be busy. Once around the corner, go right over the railway bridge, then passing on the left of Bertheos Farm (which has bed and breakfast accommodation), through two five-barred gates onto an obvious track bearing to the left. Go through another barred gate, now with views of Dolwyddelan Castle and Moel Siobad to your left. Bear right, uphill, with footpath signs on the ground to guide you, and follow the track up towards the wood's edge, over a section of stone slabs through the marshland to a sleeper footbridge and stile leading onto open ground. Continue ahead at first, then over slate slabs crossing the drainage gully, proceeding once again towards the village of Dolwyddelan. Go through the farmyard and onto a track alongside the railway.

Dolwyddelan

This village was once a thriving slate mining community, overlooked by the castle which was for a time the home of Llewelyn The Great - another Welsh patriot. If you are looking for refreshments or the railway station, bear left at the junction. If not, bear right and at the end terrace, left onto a track through the old quarrying area . The next section is over National Trust property. You might see a path leading off to the right shortly, as indicated on the Ordnance Survey. Beware of this, as it ends in a dangerous area of old quarry workings. The route suggested here seems to be preferred by most walkers joining the right of way a little further on.

Follow this forestry road for about one mile and as it begins to descend and you see a gateway and track on the left leading towards the railway and clapper bridge, bear right through a gateway and walk up what appears to be a stream bed, but which soon curves left through another gate into the wood. Bear right here up to the wood's edge, go over a stile and the path leads through bracken and pasture into the wood again. Follow this up to the moorland. Here the path seems indistinct, but soon becomes a well-trodden route, bearing slightly left towards the summit of Foel Felen, but then bearing to the right of this summit into woodland once again. There are superb views from this path and the walker enjoys a real sense of isolation among the grandeur of the mountains.

The path winds its way down through the wood to a gap in a drystone wall and over a stream to a forestry track. Turn sharp right then left down (waymarked) to the track at Ty Mawr. Turn left and follow this down the valley, continuing ahead at the forest crossroads, through a barred gate. Just beyond the cottage, go through the stone gateway onto the clear path to the footbridge.

Gethin's Bridge

Below is the fast flowing River Lledr. Before you is the solid looking viaduct built by a renowned local stonemason. Go over the footbridge and the path curves around to the left and up several steps to the main road. Turn left and go under the bridge. Bear first right, then look for a path leading off to the left into what appears to be a thick jungle, waymarked by a red arrow. Brace yourself for the steepest climb of the walk. Go up the concrete steps, bear left and continue upwards, shortly bearing left over a footbridge up to another forestry track. Cross over and continue upwards through the forest, beautifully cool on a hot summer's day. Avoid paths off to the right.

Llyn Elsi

The path emerges at Llyn Elsi, a view reminiscent of a land that time has passed by. Built in the 1920s, this reservoir serves Betws-y-Coed. Bear right onto the track but as it also bends to the right, go left along the banks of the reservoir to the obelisk. You will, in clear weather, enjoy exceptionally good views of the main Snowdon range from here. Bear right, following the green and silver markers at first. Cross over two forestry tracks continuing ahead (silver waymark) on a winding path down to another track. Bear left here. You come out behind the church in Betws-y-Coed.

The Welsh Mountain Resort

This little town is an enchanting place out of season. But it gets extremely overcrowded in summer when coach after coach arrives and a constant stream of cars makes it difficult to cross the road. But to compensate, there's a huge choice of accommodation, cafes and pubs, and a number of attractions besides, including the seven-inch gauge steam railway at the Conwy Valley Railway Museum adjacent to the British Rail Station where, if you're a little footsore, there's a train to rescue you.

Gwydir Forest

But if you are continuing to Llanrwst, turn left on the main road then right across one of Betws-y-Coed's famous bridges over the Afon Leugwy. Turn left by the toilets, then after a short distance right again (waymarked orange). As the lane curves to the right, bear left upwards before the 'Do Not Trespass' notice. This leads up to a forest track offering a good view back over Betws-y-Coed. Bear right and shortly on the left is a path which leads up to Llyn Parc, a fairly steep climb in places. At the top bear right and at the next main junction, bear first right. At the next fork, keep to the upper track which then zigzags downhill before continuing as a wide path towards Gwydir Castle once again. This meets with a forest track. Keep ahead for a short distance, then bear right down to a tarmac lane. Turn left to Gwydir Uchaf Chapel and Forestry Commission office. By the chapel there are steps down to the road. Gwydir Castle is to your right; the "castle" is really a medieval manor house, heavily restored.

Llanrwst and the Buttermilk Bridge

Your way is to the left, then right, along the road to *Bont-y-Bara Llaeth*, the Buttermilk Bridge. The old bridge had collapsed and according to the engineer, it was because the central locking stones had been placed in upside down - a piece of shoddy workmanship that had resulted from supping too much mead during the work. The replacement bridge built in 1636, reputedly to a design by Inigo Jones, was constructed this time by masons allowed to drink buttermilk only as they worked. It must have been an effective remedy because the bridge has been there ever since!

Once over the bridge, bear left into Ancester Square, then left again along Station Road where the station is to the left. This is a lovely old market town (pronounced *Lanroost*). Llewelyn the Great, one of the most famous warrior Princes of Wales who died in 1240, is buried in an enormous stone coffin in the Gwydir Chapel, in the town centre, whilst for those less poetically inclined at the end of a 13 mile tramp, there is a pub located but two minutes' gentle hobble from the railway station platform.

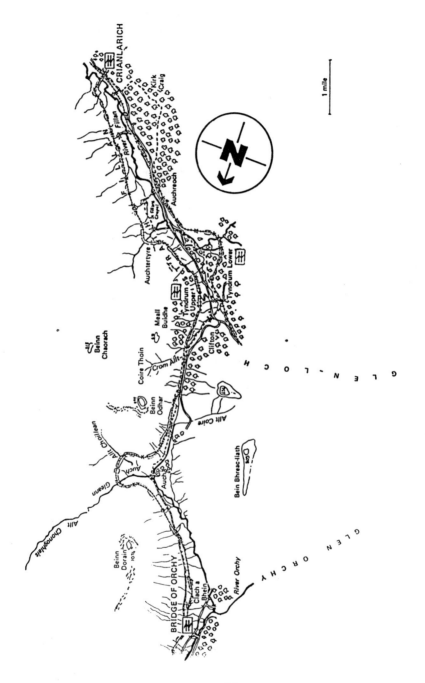

1 mile

N

CRIANLARICH

Kirk Craig

River Fillan

Auchreoch

Auchtertyre

Meall Buidhe

Beinn Chaorach

Coire Thoin

Crom Allt

Tyndrum Upper

Tyndrum Lower

Clifton

G L E N - L O C H

Beinn Odhar

Allt Coire

Bein Bhreac-liath

Allt Choillean

Gleann

Auch

Auch

Allt Chonoghais

Beinn Dorain

BRIDGE OF ORCHY

Clach a Bhein

River Orchy

G L E N   O R C H Y

WALK SEVENTEEN: The West Highland Way

Landranger map: Sheet 50. Route and map also contained in HMSO West Highland Way Route Guide

Starting Station: Crianlarich or Tyndrum (Upper or Lower)

Finishing Station: Bridge of Orchy

Distance: $13^1/2$ or 7 miles (22 or 11 kms)

Time required: 6 hours (full walk) or 3 hours (shorter version)

Grade: Moderate (full walk) or easy (shorter version).

Possible Cut-Off Point(longer walk): Tyndrum Upper or Lower.

Terrain: Well waymarked tracks and paths throughout - all this route is on the West Highland Way Long Distance Route. First section, Crianlarich-Tyndrum has some steep sections of path, and some places where the path is muddy. Second section is much easier, with good dry tracks throughout.

Refreshment and Accommodation: Facilities at Crianlarich, Tyndrum, Bridge of Orchy. Youth Hostel at Crianlarich.

Tourist Information: Fort William and Lochaber Tourist Board: (0379) 3781

THE RAIL JOURNEY

The West Highland Line between Glasgow Queen Street and Fort William offers, from a point soon after Dumbarton and the outer suburbs of Glasgow, a hundred miles of magnificent Highland scenery, with the kind of spectacular landscape which soon has passengers rushing from windows at one side of the carriage windows to the other. There is Gareloch and the sombre majesty of Loch Long, then the legendary delights of Loch Lomond, followed by the rich, semi natural forest of Glen Falloch to Crianlarich, where the Oban and Fort William lines separate, but run parallel on each side of Strath Fillan. Each has a station, at Tyndrum Upper and Lower, before the Fort William line edges its way through the Grampian Mountains, over a narrow pass into Glen Orchy. Then follows an epic piece of railway as the line climbs the vast, inhospitable expanse of Rannoch Moor, climbing to over 1, 300 feet (400 metres) above sea level at Corrour Summit before a spectacular descent through Glen Nevis to Fort William.

Near St Fillan's Chapel

This is a railway on the grand scale, superbly engineered to take advantage of the natural contours of the terrain, winding its way through the natural passes and mountain glens. It was opened in 1894, late in the railway building era. Among its many spectacular features are the great viaduct in Glen Falloch, the impressive horseshoe curve at

Auch Gleann, passed on this walk, and the crossing of Rannoch Moor, a thrilling engineering feat, with the permanent way literally floated over the bog on thick layers of brushwood, the brushwood preserved in the peat. At Cruach, north of Rannoch, there is a snow shed, the only one on a railway in the British Isles, to protect the line in the winter months from the blizzards that rage over the Moor. Even so, in the most extreme conditions, passenger trains are sometimes stranded, and emergency supplies, including food, have to be carried by train crews during the winter months. On the other hand, the trains are often the only transport available when roads are blocked with drifting snow, and the West Highland Line is a lifeline in more senses than one.

The basic three trains a day service is, as far as Tyndrum, supplemented by a similar frequency on the former Caledonian Line to Oban, giving an additional choice of trains to Crianlarich. If you are returning from Tyndrum, take care to check which station you are using - Oban trains from Tyndrum Lower, Fort William trains from Tyndrum Upper Station.

Among the delights of the West Highland line are the Swiss-style, beautifully kept stations, all brightly painted, with flowers everywhere, and the little white Highland Terrier motif on stations signs and on the side of locomotives. Because the line is single track with passing loops at many of the stations, many are still manned, and there are excellent little platform refreshment rooms at Crianlarich and, incredibly, at Rannoch where freshly ground coffee is served.

THE WALK - Crianlarich to Tyndrum and Bridge of Orchy

This walk uses Scotland's first and most popular Long Distance Route, the West Highland Way. No apologies for that. It is an excellent route along its full 95 miles (152 kilometres), with several newly created stretches of path to avoid roadwalking. The route is clearly waymarked with the little thistle logo. The section between Crianlarich and Bridge of Orchy follows the railway, closely, so the West Highland Line provides a perfect opportunity to sample the route, and it is quite certain once tasted you'll surely come back to enjoy. Though this may seem, at superficial glance, one of the least spectacular sections of the West Highland Way, dominated as the valleys are by road and railway, nothing could be further from the truth. Here the landscape has a grandeur and a majesty which the railway line, with passing trains reduced to the proportions of toys by the scale of the mountains, serves only to enhance.

Anti-Jacobite road

From Crianlarich Station, once you leave the delights of the railway refreshment room after morning coffee, cross down under the bridge, keeping left back under the line into the rather plain little village centre, heading northwest along the A82, soon passing a fine West Highland Way Information Board before going under the Oban railway line. Keep ahead for a short way along the road, but soon look for a signposted path on the left which takes the West Highland Way up a steep embankment. This becomes a pleasant path, metalled in places, crossing a burn by a tiny bridge. This is part of one of the old Military Roads built in the Highlands in the mid 18th century by General Wade and his successor as part of the process of the "pacification" of the Highlands after the Jacobite rebellions.

This path eventually climbs through young forestry, and soon joins the main line of the West Highland Way as it comes from Glen Falloch. The superb, immense peak directly to the south is An Caisteal.

The Way now turns right along a forestry path, soon climbing a rocky hillside with increasingly magnificent views in all directions, particularly down into Strath Fillan with the massive form of Ben Challum dominating the horizon, and the railway line now no more than a pencil line drawn along its immense flank.

The Way now swings northwards, descending to cross the little Herive Burn at a footbridge, and on along the forest road, gradually descending towards the A82 road. At the road, look for the path as it keeps sharp left to follow the side of the railway as it tunnels under the road. Keep along this steep line of fence, before dropping to go under a railway viaduct and along an old stretch of road, before crossing the main road at the waymarks. The path follows the embankment at the other side of the road, before turning right to cross a meadow to join the farm track leading across the River Fillan and Kirkton Farm.

St. Fillan

A clump of trees at the farm hides the ruins of St. Fillan's Chapel. St. Fillan was an Irish monk who died on Inchcailloch on Loch Lomond in 734 AD. He enjoyed miraculous powers and a Priory was established at this spot by Robert the Bruce in the 14th century. Astonishingly, two relics of the Chapel have survived, a beautiful silver Crozier (containing an even more ancient one, perhaps belonging to the Saint himself) and the Ancient Chapel Bell. Both are now kept in the National Museum of Antiquities in Edinburgh.

The Way is now a track leading from below the chapel and little graveyard, keeping ahead to Auchtertyre Farm and a bridge over the stream. Follow the farm track down to the main road. The Way goes directly across, to join the old road to the White Bridge. Avoid the temptation to cross here, the path making its way close to the riverside among pebbles, before picking up a firmer line of track which leads to a footbridge over a stream.

Caledonian Pines

The path now swings right and meanders into a beautiful section of pine wood, a fragment of the ancient Caledonian Forest, richly carpeted in pine needles. Keep ahead on the path which emerges in a caravan site just below at Tyndrum Lower Station. If you're heading for the centre of this former lead mining town (with a welcoming hotel), or indeed to the Upper Station if a return train is due on that line, the track right will take you there. Otherwise, continue in the same direction by the level crossing, along a track which veers into Clifton, an out settlement of Tyndrum. There is a shop at the main road.

Walkers planning to do only the upper section of this route can join at either Tyndrum station, directly onto the route from Tyndrum Lower, or descending the station drive from Tyndrum Upper, and turning right along the road for Clifton.

Across the Pass

From Tyndrum it is easy walking, for the most part following a stretch of old Military Road. This particular section was built between 1750 and

1752 and goes close to the stream which forms Crom Allt, past the storage tanks which provide Tyndrum's Water supply. Soon stream, railway, modern road and Military Road are competing for space in this narrow valley. Cross the railway line near the summit of the pass. Keep ahead onto a quite delightful uphill section, for a time away from the old road, a route surely designed to exploit the magnifcent views ahead of Beinn Dorain, at 1074 metres or well over 3,000 feet above sea level one of the many giants of the Grampians and a noble, distinctive peak.

The path suddenly twists sharp left, well signed, back under the railway to join the old road, and there follows a particularly lovely stretch of route, easy walking along the old track with expansive views, especially grand to the right as you look into Auch Gleann and the huge railway horseshoe over two magnificent viaducts. It's difficult to judge what is the most impressive experience - watching a train negotiating that immense curve, or travelling on a train doing just that.

Into Glen Orchy

The Way crosses the beck by Auch Farm, and heads North West, close to the railway, gradually approaching it and finally going underneath once more, then rising above it as the narrow pass is joined by the impressive gorge of Glen Orchy, richly forested. Views you hadn't imagined existed open out around you, a vast amphitheatre of hills, great craggy ranges to the north west, some of the highest summits in the British Isles. Back the way you have come, the noble peaks have a rare splendour.

Bridge of Orchy is soon reached. This is a tiny roadside hamlet on the A82, its name taken from the bridge over the River Orchy that takes Military Road on towards the notorious Glen Coe. The Way plunges directly down to the little station. No doubt you'll have carefully checked your returning train and if there's time in hand, the excellent Bridge of Orchy Hotel will have food and refreshment, and indeed accommodation, for all tastes.

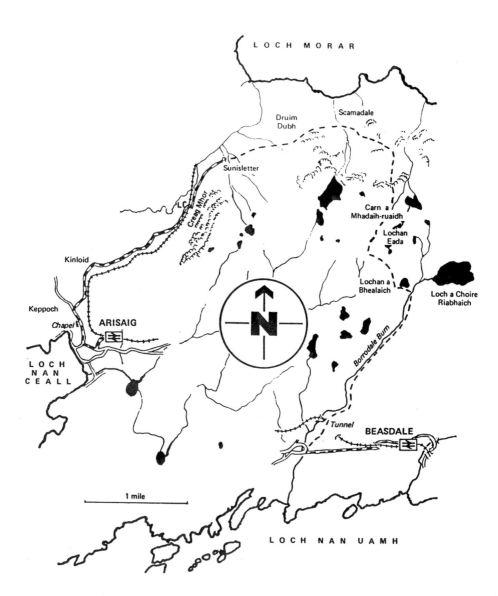

LOCH MORAR

Scamadale

Druim
Dubh

Sunisletter

Creag Mhor

Carn a
Mhadaih-ruaidh

Lochan
Eada

Kinloid

Lochan a
Bhealaich

Loch a Choire
Riabhaich

Keppoch

Chapel

ARISAIG

N

LOCH
NAN
CEALL

Borrodale Burn

Tunnel

BEASDALE

1 mile

LOCH NAN UAMH

WALK EIGHTEEN: The Road to the Isles

Landranger Map: Sheet 40

Pathfinder Map: Sheet NM 68/78

Starting Station: Beasdale

Finishing Station: Arisaig

Distance: 8 miles (13kms)

Time required: 5 hours

Grade: Strenuous.

Possible Cut-Off Point: Lochan a Bhealaigh

Terrain: Paths through rough heather and moorland, not visible on ground for much of the route. Some difficult pathfinding - compass, large scale map essential. A stream has to be forded. This route is not recommended for inexperienced walkers or in bad weather.

Easy or bad weather alternative: Remain on train to Arisaig. Follow road to Kinloid, then farm track to Sunisletter and Scamadale. Return same route (8 miles, 13km easy, level walking on tracks).

Refreshment, accommodation facilities: The Arisaig Hotel, Arisaig.

Tourist Information: Highland, Fort William (0397) 3781

THE RAIL JOURNEY

The Mallaig section of West Highland line must be one of the most
beautiful railway lines in the world, rivalled in Britain only by its near
neighbour - the Kyle of Lochalsh. For sheer romantic splendour, the
landscape is quite breathtaking. The line's $41^1/_2$ miles have got
everything - mountains, rivers, lochs, gorges, and even coastline - for the
last ten miles or so, it skirts the Atlantic ocean. At Glen Finnan, the
railway crosses a magnificent viaduct directly behind that noble
monument to one of great lost causes of history, the point where Bonny
Prince Charlie and his Highlanders first raised the flag of the ill-fated
Jacobite Rebellion in 1745.

Lochan a Bhealaich, Beasdale

In railway terms, the Mallaig Line has a very recent history. It was only
opened by the North British Railway in 1901. From the very beginning
the Government recognised its enormous social and economic value to
the crofting and fishing communities of the thinly populated Highlands,
offering substantial financial guarantees to the railway company for the
building of the line and cash grants for the pier and breakwater at

Mallaig. So the concept of the "social railway" goes right back to Edwardian times in the Scottish Highlands.

Building of the line was less of a problem because of the easy access for men and materials by water, on adjacent sea lochs. There are few tunnels, but some spectacular engineering features nonetheless, including deep cuttings, and stretches with a ruling gradient of 1 in 40 that make even the powerful Class 37 locomotives growl. The contractor was a famous engineering name, Robert McAlpine of Glasgow, whose great concrete viaduct at Glen Finnan was a brilliant use of a relatively new material, a technology exploited by later generations in the building of the road network. McAlpine's have kept a close interest in the West Highland line and have been closely associated with the restoration of regular steam-hauled services on the line during the summer months.

As on the West Highland line further south, stations have brightly painted wooden shingles with red shale on the platforms, well tended flower beds and pots, and the cheerful White Highland Terrier on stations signs and on the sides of the ubiquitous Class 37 locomotives.

The line is served by a basic morning, mid-day and evening train service that links with trains south from Fort William, including the London sleepers. To enjoy the line at its best, and to have time to do a walk, you must stay overnight at Fort William, and catch the morning train which soon trundles out of the shadow of Ben Nevis, Britain's highest mountain, around the head of Loch Linnhe and along the side of Loch Eil. The line then ascends to the head of Glen Finnan, past the Monument, forcing its way through the wild, mountainous glen of Abhainn Shlatach, all crags and heather, with spectacular views from both sides of the carriage windows, before coming down to the shores of Loch Eilt. It then twists and meanders through a landscape of indescribable beauty, passing Loch Ailort, Loch Dubh and Loch Nan Uamh, the last really a sea inlet, filled with scattered islands, before turning northwards up the Arisaig Peninsular for Morar and Mallaig. The beach at Loch Nan Uamh, near Borrodale, earns a footnote in history being the point where Prince Charles Edward Stuart first landed on July 18th 1745 from a French ship. You will see the landing place and a commemorative cairn on an islet, shortly before arriving at Beasdale Station.

THE WALK - Borrodale and Loch Morar

Though this is a rough, wild walk, with tricky pathfinding, the views can only be described as superlative, a mixture of heather moorland, woodland and stunningly beautiful coastline, along sea lochs, over to the islands of Eig, Muck and Rhum, and the mountains of Skye itself. Because you cross a little peninsular, with a quite steep ascent (almost 1500 feet or 450 metres from sea level) you enjoy these views in three different directions. Save this walk up for a fine, bright day, perhaps in spring or in autumn, when the heather is purple, and it will be a quite unforgettable experience.

Alight at Beasdale Halt. You must make your request to the train guard well in advance otherwise the train doesn't stop. From the station turn left into the main A830 (more a lane by English standards) walking through a lovely area of woodland, under the railway bridge and down a good mile towards Arisaig House, where the road bears sharply to the right. Before the bend and de-restriction signs look for a field-gate on the right. Across the narrow field is another field gate leading into a wood.

This is your path. Cross the field, to the gate and the wood. You'll find traces of a path in the wood, winding between the rhododendron and pine. Keep the same direction uphill, with luck picking up the line of the narrow path in the wood. It emerges at the top of the wood, veering left above the wood, before swinging slightly right to cross through a tall deer fence at a gate.

Borrodale

You are now in open heather moor, and will soon pick up a narrow but clear path which follows Borrodale Burn uphill, heading in a Northeasterly direction along the right hand side of the Burn. Once you're on this path, the route is easy to follow for the next two miles, a steep climb, occasionally crossing a little gully (usually with a bridging plank) never more than about 50 metres from the stream, sometimes much closer. As you climb, quite superb views open out behind you, southwards, over Loch nan Uamh, a panorama of coastline, islands, mountains. This is an exceptionally fine climb, following the little gully up, occasionally contouring round, superb views behind. Not far past a narrow crossing stream, Coire an Eas Bhain, you ascend a broad breast of moorland, the stream in a steep gully to your left, before descending into a shallow hollow or corrie. Ahead, beyond the fence, is Loch a Choire Riabhaich. The path peters out around here, and one narrow way heads towards the fence. Your way is, however, over the stream to the left. This is only a narrow mountain stream but too broad to stride or scramble across, and except in the driest weather (rare in the Highlands) you'll have to wade across. It's not deep, but the current is strong, so take care, and decide whether it's best to carry your boots and paddle, or put up with wet feet and wade.

Once across, you'll pick up the line of path again to the lovely Lochan a Bhealaich. Though by now you will have done most of the climbing, a strong walker will require a minimum of 3 hours for the remainder of the route, so if you're planning to catch the teatime train back, this is the point to return - or even before the ford - if you haven't that time in hand, or the weather has turned poor.

Views of Skye

In fact, the little Loch, a superb, perfect little circle of water set in the heather and moorgrass, is well worth getting your feet wet for, a little jewel. The path goes along the south side, soon ascending a little knoll, from where there is another tremendous viewpoint, looking right along the Arisaig peninsular, that wild, rocky landscape, with the coast and islands in the background, Skye ahead, and, if you're in luck, a herd of red deer on the foreground. Avoid the temptation to be drawn downhill into this landscape. There is no path on the ground. Your route lies North West, along the contours. Look at the map carefully. You must traverse round along the top of a broad, shallow valley for about half a mile (1 km), looking for a natural pass through the hills. The only landmarks are the contours on the map, and you are heading for a shallow natural pass on your right. Bearing due north with the lie of the land you will come to a deer fence and a gate - the gate indicating the lie of the path. Go through here, across the summit of the pass and, in a short distance, you enjoy another great moment - this time the huge expanse of Loch Morar, dark blue or black, depending on the weather, ahead of you. Loch Morar is the deepest lake in Britain, more than 1,000 feet - 330 metres - in places. Particularly lovely are the hamlets and farms scattered along the loch shore, and the pale sand of the little beaches.

Scamadale

Your descent is basically down the narrow valley ahead, all the way down enjoying this superb panoramic view. The burn indicates the way, as do a pair of landrover tracks. Keep the burn to your right, following the tracks as they meander, unbelievably steeply, down the hill shoulder on the side of Carn a Mhadaidh. This is not a difficult way to follow, though the path vanishes in places. Soon you leave the burn across open fellside, bearing slightly left - the white farm of Scamadale becomes a bearing point ahead. You'll pick up the path again, now to the left of another narrow burn, twisting and plunging down, swinging steeply left. You cross the edge of an area of new forestry, then down a very steep slope to Scamadale, a forester's cottage and outpost of civilisation close to a shallow bay on Loch Morar.

From Scamadale this is a very different kind of walk, along an easy, stony farm track, no pathfinding problems, soon curving over the little partially wooded peninsular of Druim Dubh and the farm at Sunisletter. Proceed ahead now to the level crossing over the West Highland Line, following the track which parallels the railway, passing a little farm before reaching the hamlet of Kinloid where the tarmac road begins. A short ascent now to the main road into Arisaig, a most beautiful little village and port for boats to the inner islands. The little Catholic Church of St. Mary's you pass on the road into the village, stands next to the medieval church of Kilmory it replaced, with its ancient burial ground a direct link with the "Old Faith".

At the cross roads the lane left leads directly to Arisaig Station; the village which lies on the main road ahead has a shop, a post office and the welcoming Arisaig Hotel.

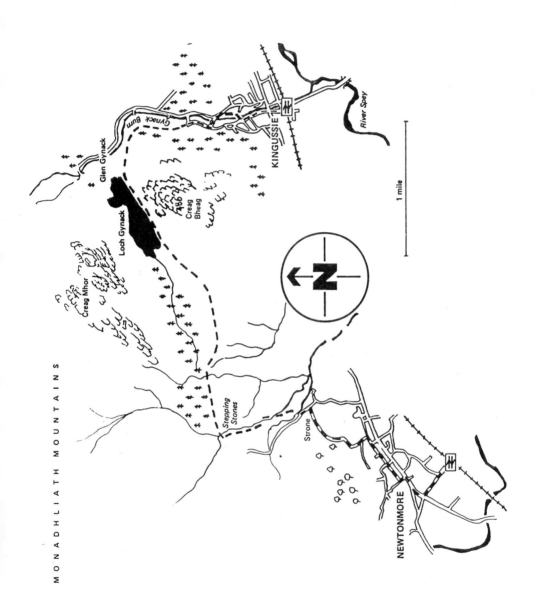

MONADHLIATH MOUNTAINS

Creag Mhor

Glen Gynack

Gynack Burn

Loch Gynack

Creag Bheag

186

KINGUSSIE

River Spey

1 mile

N

Stepping Stones

Strone

NEWTONMORE

WALK NINETEEN: Loch Gynack

Landranger Map: Sheet 35

Pathfinder Maps: Sheets NH 60/70, NN69/79

Starting Station: Kingussie

Finishing Station: Newtonmore

Distance: 6 miles (10kms)

Time required: 3 hours

Grade: Easy.

Possible Cut-Off Point: Loch Gynack

Terrain: Lane, woodland and fieldpaths to Loch Gynack; beyond Loch Gynack open moorland, with some boggy areas where boots essential. Walkers without suitable footwear should return from Loch Gynack by the same route - a good wet weather alternative.

Refreshment and accommodation facilities: Both Kingussie and Newtonmore have a good choice of inns, cafes, bed and breakfast facilities. Youth Hostel in Kingussie. Wednesday is early closing in both Newtonmore and Kingussie.

Tourist Information: Main Road, Aviemore (0479) 810363

THE RAIL JOURNEY

The Perth-Inverness line is to Scotland what the Settle to Carlisle line is to England - its most spectacular main line, ascending as it does from the rich, rolling countryside north of Perth, through the awesome Pass of

Killiecrankie to Pitlochry and Blair Atholl. It then climbs through Glen Garry to the desolate wastes of Dalnaspidal, and the Pass of Drumochter, at 1,484 feet above sea level the highest main line in the British Isles - though it shares the pass with the busy A9. Then comes the long descent past Dalwhinnie itself, with its lineside whisky distillery (at 1,188 feet, the highest in the world), into Strathspey, a deep narrow gorge between the massive Cairngorm mountain peaks, many of them over 4,000 (1,200 metres) high. The line curves past Newtonmore, Kingussie and Aviemore, now an international winter sports centre, where the little Strathspey Railway, a privately operated steam railway, runs at weekends and during the summer holiday period from Speyside Station for 5^1/$_2$ miles to Boat of Garten along a short surviving branch of Highland Railway line from Aviemore to Forres.

Near Strome, Strathspey

Beyond Aviemore, the main line continues through a lovely forested landscape to Carrbridge, named after the Bridge of Carr over the River Dulnran, built in 1717, before swinging sharply westwards and beginning a long, gradual descent via Daviot and Culloden, site of the terrible battle of 1746, to Inverness, through countryside which loses little in grandeur. With through rail services from Glasgow, Edinburgh and London, this dramatically beautiful railway is a lifeline in more sense than one to the Cairngorm Region, both for local needs and in bringing considerable numbers of tourists into the region for both summer walking and sightseeing and winter skiing. Because of the terrain, much of the route is single track, yet such crack trains as the High Speed "Highland Chieftain" and "The Clansman" and the night sleeper "Royal Highlander" roar over what is a superbly engineered line.

Most trains stop at Kingussie. Newtonmore, however, has a more restricted service, so please check return times carefully before planning this walk.

THE WALK

Kingussie, a small mountain resort, is well supplied with facilities. Make time if you can to visit the Highland Folk Museum with its wide range of outdoor exhibits. There is plenty of time to fit this in before this short walk. The museum is open from 10am every day, except Sundays. There's also opportunity in the vicinity, for superb high level walks in the Cairngorms. This particular walk is a mere taster, designed to avoid any worry about train times, but it nevertheless offers some superb views of the major mountain ranges, most notably the magnificent ridge culminating in A'Chailleach (930 metres) which dominates the latter part of the walk, and forms an outlier of the great Monadhliath Mountains to the west.

Glen Gynack

From the station follow the road, left, to the cross roads on the old A9 in the town centre - a quieter road than in the recent past thanks to the new by-pass. Cross directly ahead to follow Gynack road at the side of the Duke of Gordon Hotel. Keep ahead up this lane, noticing the stream and waterfall on the right. A short distance up the road look for a gap on the right which leads to a path descending steps to a wooden footbridge over the stream. Cross, ascending the other side before turning left by a bench, and following the path along the riverside. This is Glen Gynack, an attractively wooded little side valley of Strathspey, with, as you ascend, dramatic views down into the steep, rocky glen, half hidden by birch, rowan and poplars.

The path emerges alongside a garden fence at the road. Turn left here, continue to a No Through Road sign where, almost immediately afterwards you see steps again descending the glen, crossing another attractive bridge by rocky pools and falls before returning up to the road.

Go right here, continuing towards a caravan site by the golf house. Go straight ahead, left of the golf house and through the caravans, at the far side of which you will find a stile which leads onto the golf course. Keep directly ahead here, following the very edge of the golf course and taking great care to avoid taking a more obvious path over a stile left into the wood. Your way follows the little beck by the edge of the golf course, crossed by the occasional footbridge, at the edge of the birch and the bracken, keeping off the greens. Where the woodland begins to swing sharply round to the right, look for a narrow path through the bracken, slightly left, which climbs upwards, still the keeping the same general direction, marked by an occasional little post. Bear right at a fork in the path to the higher green, walk to the left and around this green to reach a high stile in the deer fence - itself a fine viewpoint back down into the valley behind.

Heather and Birch

The way is now across open moorland, a clear, narrow path between the heather which bears left out of the head of Glen Gynack up to the shores of Loch Gynack, an exquisitely beautiful mountain tarn, the far side of which is overlooked by the steep crag of Creag Mhor reflecting into the water. The near side, through which the path meanders, is a beautiful heather and birch woodland, a kind of natural mountain garden.

No doubt you'll want to dawdle a little here, enjoying the superb views of lake and mountain. The path continues alongside the lake, along a shelf above the shoreline. As the vegetation thins out, the path bears slightly left, ascending the shoulder of a steep little peak to the left, Creag Bhead, eventually merging with a faint path from that peak's summit which, for those with time and energy to spare, offers a superb panoramic view of the Spey Valley with the massive Cairngorm peaks as a backcloth.

But the main path continues directly ahead down to a gateway ahead. Go through here. This is where a little careful pathfinding is needed because away from the path, wet and boggy places exist. But if you keep directly ahead, you'll pick up the faint lines of a moorland track which will carry you safely through the treacherous ground (boots are in any case essential for this section of the walk). This track veers across to the forest on the right where, at a gate, it enters the forest through a narrow gap.

Your way is to ford a narrow and steep stream to the left, and, roughly following the outside wall of the forest, pick your path carefully through the heather. Watch out for several wet places, but with care and some meandering, you'll reach another gate, a little difficult to open (untwist the wire and close it behind you), which goes under the high deer fence.

This is deer stalking country and during the main season (August-October), you are requested to keep to paths and avoid disturbing the shoot.

Mountain Views

The path crosses the stream directly ahead, and the remnants of a footbridge too far gone for to be any use. There are some residual stepping stones, but crossing can be quite a problem if the burn is in spate. If so, do not despair, but stay on the same bank, walking about half a mile downstream past another lethal and rotting bridge, past the waterworks cottage, to finally reach a firm and secure bridge. This joins the same moorland paths and track which meander along the far bank at a slightly higher level, fording another narrow stream, easy to stride. Because of its greater height the path on the far bank has finer views - a great panorama of hills which, early and late in the year will have snow on the summits and, if the weather is clear you'll enjoy a spectacular sight.

Head for the gate in the wall ahead to where the track emerges on a lane by a little ruined cottage. Turn right through the hamlet of Strone, and descend into Newtonmore. Right at the first junction then left to the main street along the old A9. Turn right through the town.

Newtonmore is another pleasant, unpreposessing Strathspey town, with a choice of inns, cafes, shops and bed and breakfast places. In the days before the railways it was an important droving centre, with one of the largest cattle markets in Scotland. If you've time, make sure you visit the Clan Macpherson Museum, filled with memorabilia of one of the most remarkable local Clans with links with the 1745 rebellion. Entrance is free of charge and it is open daily throughout the summer. But allow a good 20 minutes from the town centre to the railway station, which is reached by following the main road southwestwards, branching left along the B9150 towards Dalwhinnie, then first left along the lane to the little Highland Railway Station with its single track line, and station verandah where you should at least find somewhere to sit till your train arrives.

DUIRINISH

Achnandarac

Allt Dhuirinish

Loch A chaidh
na h-Inich

Torr
Fhionn

Cnoc
Chlarsair

Carn Thollaidh

Cnoc a
Chlarsair

Sgurr Beag

Loch
Palascaig

Loch Iain
Oig

Coille Mhor

Loch
Scalpaich

Coillemore

Carn na
Snaobhaig

KYLE OF LOCHALSH

piers

KYLE

ferry

AKIN

LOCH ALSH

Kyleakin

1 mile

SKYE

WALK TWENTY: Kyle of Lochalsh

Landranger Maps: Sheet 24 and Sheet 33

Pathfinder Maps: Sheets 72/73, 82/92, 83/93

Starting Station: Duirinish

Finishing Station: Kyle of Lochalsh

Distance: $8^1/_2$ Miles (14 kms)

Time required: 4 hours

Grade: Moderate-Strenuous.

Possible Cut-Off Point: Loch Achaidh na h-Inich $2^1/_2$ miles (4km).

Terrain: A mixture of reasonable paths and rough heather, moor grass and even boggy land. Some tricky pathfinding and care needed on the central sections - a walk for experienced ramblers able to orienteer from a map.

Refreshment and accommodation facilities: Kyle of Lochalsh - cafes, station bar, shops, hotel.

Easy or bad weather alternative: Follow lane south from crossroads beyond Duirinish village for 2 miles then left at cross roads past Lochs Ian Oig and Pelascaig then as text - 6 miles, 3 hours required.

Tourist Information: Church Street, Inverness (0463) 23435 *or* Portree, Isle of Skye (0748) 2137

THE RAIL JOURNEY

The Kyle line, like the Mallaig section of the Western Highland line, must be one of the most beautiful railway journeys in Western Europe. Its 82 miles cut right across Scotland from the North Sea Coast to the Atlantic, and the traveller enjoys views which become ever more spectacular.

The Kyle of Lochalsh

From Inverness, the line follows the edge of the great coastal inlet of Beauly Firth, before turning northwards through the narrow gap of land between the hills that leads into Cromarty Firth. At Dingwall, the Kyle line separates from the Wick line to begin its long journey westwards, climbing through the mountains and some of the most thinly populated areas of Western Europe - across Strathpeffer to Garve, by Loch Luichart, Achanalt and Achnasheen, all mere hamlets close to rail halts. Then follows the long, lovely descent through Glen Carron, along the little River Carron through a narrow niche between mountains over 3,000 feet (1,000 metres) high, by Achnashellach and Loch Dughaill, and soon by the shores of Loch Carron, a vast sea loch leading into the Atlantic ocean. If the ride so far has been magnificent, the last 20 miles develop into something quite magical, the railway skirting the very edge of the loch, the mountains, mainly forested, rising steeply up behind, hauntingly beautiful.

Stromeferry, the terminus of the line between 1870 and 1897, until the extension to Kyle was completed, had a brief period of glory again in the 1970s when the oil platform building industry was at its height, because of its deep water wharf. Now once again the sidings rust and the jetties decay. But as the line, with its cuttings and tortuous curves, which cost £20,000 per mile to construct in the 1890s, edges its way by the mouth of Loch Carron, the view from the carriage window (be sure to sit on the right hand side) becomes ever more spectacular, with islands, rocky inlets, across to the shores of Applecross. Soon you reach the hamlet of Plockton, the "jewel" of the Kyle line, almost a Mediterranean village, the white and colour wash houses reflecting into the waters of a sheltered cove. The final miles past Duirinish into Kyle of Lochalsh itself, the little station by the jetty for the Skye Ferry, are dominated by the mountains on the Isle of Skye. The little town at Kyle of Lochalsh, with a population of 600, grew up entirely as a result of the railway and its port, and many businesses in the town are dependent on the line, the visitors and other trade the railway brings.

The line was built in stages until finally opened by the Highland Railway on November 2nd 1897, thanks to a grant of £45,000 from the Government towards the enormous construction costs and in recognition of the contribution the line would make to the fishing industry and for the carrying of mail in this otherwise isolated area.

The social importance of the Kyle Line came to the fore again in the 1970s when, because of rising costs, the line was considered for closure. However, the inability of bus services to cope with traffic congestion in summer and winter conditions, plus widespread opposition to closure proposals, led the Government to agree to provide continued support, with the line now being increasingly valued for its contribution to the tourist development of the region, particularily for visitors from overseas.

THE WALK

Alight at Duirinish Station, an unstaffed request stop. One reason for choosing this station for a walk was to allow opportunity to the whole of this remarkable line to be travelled. Present timetables permit the walk to be completed by a reasonably strong walker between mid day arriving and teatime departing trains, but if you want to take your time to savour the scenic splendours, either catch the earlier train or arrange to stay overnight in Kyle - or even on Skye, only a short ferry crossing away.

Loch Achaidh

Follow the track along the station drive into Duirinish village, forking left over the stream bridge and keeping ahead by cottages through this little settlement to the main road. Go left here, but take the first turn right signed to Achnadarack. After about 200 metres, shortly beyond a bridge over a stream, take the stile on the right which leads into a wood. Descend to a small stream, crossed by a little footbridge, and follow the path up the stream, the Allt Dhuirinish.

According to the map this path follows the stream directly up to join a broad forestry track to Loch Achaidh. It is, however, somewhat overgrown, and a more obvious track bears off left up a shallow knoll. This track soon dips down to ford a stream and rejoin the road. If you take this way, turn right along the road, a lovely wooded stretch, to a crossroads, where you bear right following the signs to Achnadarach, a group of handsome houses. If you managed to trace the direct path, however, this emerges as a broad forestry track on the same lane about 200 metres further east. Keep on the lane to the lake, the Loch Achaidh na h-Inich.

A path goes left around this loch, soon crossing a wooden bridge over the stream, and becoming a beautiful lochside path, a superb mixture of still water, woodland and mountain, a splendid and atmospheric place.

Mountain Pass

Keep on the path, through a gate, around the edge of the loch which, after such a promising start, begins to peter out and cross an area of soft and boggy land at the head of the loch. Keep in the same direction with care and you will see remnants of footbridges across the crossing becks, though you'll be lucky not to get your feet damp (faint hearts return here). Keep ahead in the same direction through scrubland, between dwarf trees. You are heading through the gap you will see between the two sharp peaks ahead, a natural pass or saddle through the hills.

The path will now have completely vanished, and though it originally appears to vanish through a gate into the Forest, your best route, and one used by other walkers, is to follow the tall Forestry Commission Fence, which you will find marked by a thin red line on the Landranger Map, climbing up through the thin woodland. This is an easy climb, but pick your way carefully, sometimes close to the fence, sometimes a few yards away as the lie of the land and vegetation dictate, heading almost due south. You soon come off the edge of the sheet of your Landranger or Pathfinder Map almost exactly between figures 81 and 82 - a kilometre apart. But as you reach the summit of the pass, you'll actually pick up the line of path once more, just below the little peak marked as Cnoc a Chlarsair.

Careful pathfinding is required here. Follow the path as it contours round the hill summit. As you come round the hillside, you will be greeted by superb open views across Loch Alsh which is, of course, the straits between the mainland and Skye, whose massive bulk stretches ahead of you, tantalisingly close. A crag ahead marks the line of path, but avoid the temptation to be drawn onto sheep paths back up the hillside. You should be heading due west, keeping above the steep hillside, to the lovely little birchwood covering the slope of the hill straight ahead. A fairly broad and obvious path, probably more used by sheep than humans, goes into the wood. Once in the wood, keep contouring round for 100 metres or so, then look for a way to your left which zigzags down the slope, close by the stream coming down from Carn Thollaidh. Keep your eyes carefully on the ground ahead, and with a little more luck you'll find another good, clear path, beautifully engineered around the slope. This swings round in a gigantic loop, above the little valley on the left, turning southwards. Irritatingly, this path once again vanishes, but keep due south, heading towards the sweep of Balmacara Bay now clearly visible ahead, and towards a little enclosure or sheep fold that will come into sight.

You'll need to dip down to cross a stream, but, on the right of the sheepfold, through gorse, you reach a good clear track down to the road by Collemore Farm.

Enjoy a well earned sense of relief - the rest of the walk is simple. Follow the lane right, uphill to the cross roads, bearing left here along the minor road which soon passes two more attractive little lochs - Loch Iain Oig and Loch Palascaig. About a quarter of a mile past Palascaig, beyond a sharp bend in the road, look for a narrow path, left, signposted to Loch Scalpaidh. This soon winds its way onto open moorland, through heather.

This is a beautiful area of National Trust for Scotland moorland, and the loch, when you reach it, is set like a desolate jewel in the open hillside, an expanse of water in a shallow bowl of the hills.

Make your way around the very narrow path that you'll find around the eastern bank. At one point, it goes down to the water's edge, and you must ford a shallow streamlet into the loch. But keep ahead to the far edge of the lake where, you'll find suddenly emerging, out of nowhere, a path heading due South West through the heather. Follow this. This curves out of the shallow hollow, bearing first left, but soon right, downhill, then curving to the other side of the shallow valley, heading to the side of the woodland ahead, again with superb views. It drops down now, through the wood, zigzagging rather thrillingly to emerge on a steep slope above the main A87 Kyle of Lochalsh road. Follow the path as it zigzags down to a small layby at the side of the road.

Just a little less than a mile, now, along the main road. If you're having to cope with the summer traffic, keep into the verge, but as you ascend the brow of a little hill, you'll soon be compensated by views of the little harbour of Kyle of Lochalsh, ferry boats chugging across from Kyleakin on Skye, freighters tied up on the wharfs, and beyond, the huge sweep of the Inner Sound, with the scattered islands and the massive Applecross peninsular in the background.

You'll probably see your train, with its familiar Class 37 locomotive and three or four coaches, waiting in the little station, surely one of the most romantically situated in the British Isles. But there must surely be time, before catching that train, to enjoy well some earned refreshment in the station buffet or elsewhere in town .

INDEX

Fort William, 128, 137
Freshwater East, 102
Fryup Dales, 87

Garburn Pass, 75, 79
Gareloch, 128
Geraldus Cambrensis, 103
Giggleswick, 59, 70
Glan Conwy, 121
Glen Carron, 152
Glen Coe, 132
Glen Falloch, 128, 130
Glen Finnan, 136
Glen Nevis, 128
Glen Orchy, 132
Glynde, 27, 27
Glyndebourne Opera, 27
Glyndwr's Way, 108
Grantham Canal, 54
Grantham, 51
Great Fryup Dale, 87
Great Northern Railway, 54
Great Western Railway, 10, 106
Great Yarmouth, 32, 35, 35
Gwydir Forest, 124
Gwynedd, 120
Gynack, Loch, 143

Halvergate, 33
Harlech, 115
Hathersage, 61
Haydon Bridge, 93
Heart of Wales Line, 105
Henry VIII, 29
Herodsfoot, 11, 12
Hexham, 92
Heyop, 109
Highland Railway, 153
Hollin Cross, 64
Hope Bowdler, 48
Hope Valley Line, 61
Hope Valley, The, 59
Housman, A. E., 46

Ingleborough, 70
Inverness, 144, 152
Ipswich, 31
Isle of Wight, 17

Jacobite rebellion, 136

Kent, River, 77
Kentmere Hall, 79
Kentmere Valley, 78
Kentmere, 75

Killiecrankie, Pass of, 143
Kingham, 37, 39, 39
Kingussie, 144
Knucklas, 109
Kyle Line, 151
Kyle of Lochalsh, 151

Ladybower Reservoir, 62
Lake District National Park, 77
Lampeter Vale, 101
Lantern Saints, 89
Lealholm, 88
Leeds-Settle-Carlisle line, 67
Leeds-Skipton-Morecambe line, 67
Lewes, 24, 27, 28, 29
Liskeard and Caradon Railway Company, 11
Liskeard and Looe Union Canal, 11
Liskeard, 11
Little Fryup Dale, 87
Little John, 62
Little North Western, 68
Llanbister, 107
Llandecwyn, 113
Llandrindod, 107, 106
LLanelli, 106
Llangammarch Wells, 107
Llangynllo, 107, 108
Llanrwst, 125
Llanwrtyd, 107
Lledr Valley, 122
Lledr, River, 123
Llewelyn The Great, 123
Llyn Elsi, 124
Loch Carron, 153
Loch Gynack, 143
Loch Lomond, 128
Loch Morar, 139
Lochalsh, Kyle of, 151
London and North Western Railway, 106
Long Man, The, 25
Long Mynd, The, 48
Looe, 13
Losehill, 63
Lyke Wake Walk, 84

Macpherson clan, 147
Mallaig, 135
Mam Tor, 64
Manorbier, 101, 103
Marches, The, 44
McAlpine, Robert, 137
Mendip Hills, 9
Merlin, 100
Middlesborough, 83
Mills, 34